HORSE TRIVIA

A

HIPPOFILE'S DELIGHT

Deborah Eve Rubin

Horse Trivia: A Hippofile's Delight

©1995 Deborah Eve Rubin

Rubin, Deborah Eve, 1954–
  Horse trivia: a hippofile's delight/Deborah Eve Rubin.
  p.   cm.   Includes index.
  ISBN 0-939481-45-6

Published in the United States of America by

Half Halt Press, Inc.
P.O. Box 67
Boonsboro, MD 21713

Cover and interior design by Graphics Plus.
Typesetting by Sutter Design, Inc.

Dedication

To the memory of Princess ("Priney," 1971–1994),

And for Chief.

Acknowledgements

All photos not otherwise credited are by the author.

The "B.C." cartoon , ©1991, is used by permission of Johnny Hart and Creators Syndicate, Inc.

The "Middle Class Animals" cartoons are ©1970. I was unable to locate the copyright holder; if you are out there, please contact me.

Thanks to the following people and companies for the information they provided:

Frank Lessiter of *The American Farriers Journal.*

Mari Kay L. Bass of the Arabian Horse registry of America, Inc.

Kim Steinman of the American Quarter Horse Association.

Some of the art in this book came from the following books published by Dover Publications of New York, and is used by permission:

Horses & Horse-Drawn Vehicles (Grafton)

Old-Time Circus Cuts (Fox)

Horses and Other Animals in Motion (Muybridge)

American Carriages, Sleighs, Sulkies and Carts (Berkebile)

Table of Contents

Frontnotes

Friar, Stephen and Ferguson, John. Basic Heraldry. New York: Norton, 1993

Frost, Murray. "Judaica Philately." Global Stamp News, issue 43 (Feb. 1994), p.30-31

Furnas, J.C. The Americans — A Social History of the United States 1587-1914. New York: Putnam, 1969

Gies, Frances and Joseph. Cathedral, Forge and Waterwheel: Technology and Invention in the Middle Ages. New York: Harper-Collins, 1994

Grousset, Ren. (trans. Naomi Walford) The Empire of the Steppes a History of Central Asia. New Brunswick, NJ: Rutgers University Press, 1970

Howey, M. Oldfield. The Horse in Magic and Myth. New York: Castle, 1958

Kirk, G.S. The Nature of Greek Myths. Harmondsworth, Middlesex, England: Penguin, 1974

Maslow, Jonathan. Sacred Horses. The Memoirs of a Turkmen Cowboy. New York: Random House, 1994

Spring, Christopher. African Arms and Armor. Washington, D.C.: Smithsonian Institution, 1993

Wilford, John Noble. "Ancient Clay Horse is Found in Syria." The New York Times, 3 Jan. 1993, p.10 (International section)

General & Miscellaneous Trivia

■ Biological classification of the horse:
kingdom *Animalia*
section *Deuterostomia*
phylum *Chordata*
subphylum *Vertebrate*
class *Mammalia*
subclass *Theria*
superorder *Mesaxonia*
order *Perissodactyla* (odd-toed ungulates; at this stage related
    to the rhinoceros and the tapir who, with the horse, are the
    only remaining families in this order. There were more than
    15 in prehistoric times.)
suborder *Hippomorpha*
superfamily *Equoidea* (only group in suborder)
genus *Equidae*
    subgenus *Equus* (true horses; the domestic horse is *Equus
    caballus)*
    subgenus *Hippotigris* (zebras)
    subgenus *Dolichohippus* (zebras)
    subgenus *Asinus* (African asses)
    subgenus *Hemionus* (Asian asses)

■ All odd-toed ungulates are descended from Lower Tertiary
Phenacondontids, in the order *Condylarthra.* All equines are
descended from the Lower Eocene genus *Hyracotherium.*

■ Horses don't have a gall bladder.

■ The wild horse of ice age Europe — basically the same animal
as the Przewalski horse — was hunted for food by ice age
humans. A major kill site during the Upper Paleolithic (about
40,000 years ago) was at Solutré, near Lyon, France. Massive

quantities of horse bones have been found there. There is some evidence that the process of domestication had begun by this time. A horse head carved out of bone has engraving on it that looks like a rope halter. It was found at St Michel d'Arudy, Basses-Pyrénées, France, in 1893. In the 1960s an Upper Paleolithic carving of a horse head wearing a halter was found at La Marche, France.

■ Horses died out in North America toward the end of the Pliestocene (between 3 million–10,000 years ago) but it's not known for sure why. Hunting by humans may have been a factor, but not a major one — no kill sites have been found for horses although horses are the most commonly found fossil in the U.S. It is more likely that radical changes in the environment were to blame.

■ The horse was domesticated late in prehistoric times, after such animals as sheep and goats.

■ Horses adapt their behavior to the environment, rapidly shedding all traces of domestication when released to the wild.

■ In the wild, foals will suckle until they are a year old, even longer in some conditions.

■ Horses on barrier islands have been observed to drink saltwater. (One famous example of barrier islands is Chincoteague and Assateague, off the Virginia and Maryland coasts, original home of Marguerite Henry's famous Misty.)

■ The most universally common form of equine society is the harem group, a band of mares dominated by one stallion. Mares often work to keep the group together even after their stallion dies. The wild asses and Grevy's zebra of Kenya lack this binding, as do some feral Australian horses. Unattached males, age three and up, travel in bachelor groups until they can form or take over a harem.

■ When a horse raises its head, draws back its upper lip and wrinkles its nostrils, the gesture is called *flehmen*. It is seen more often in males, especially stallions, than females. Flehmen is thought to be a way to direct scents in the air to specialized olfactory glands at the end of the nasal passage.

■ In the feral ("wild") horses of the American west, it has been observed that when a stallion takes over a harem, it will induce abortions in those mares already pregnant, often by raping them. This frees the mares to bear his foals, passing on his genetic heritage rather than that of the stallion he vanquished. It's not known if this is a recent behavior or one that has existed for centuries.

■ Stallions will fight over females, but generally not over territory.

■ Horses have memories that put elephants to shame.

■ A horse's teeth occupy more space in its head than its brain.

■ The approximate gestation period of the horse is 337 days.

■ The horse has the largest eyes of any land animal.

■ Horses are not color-blind.

■ Horses have binocular vision, but can also see different things with each eye. Which is why you've got to make sure that your horse sees all the spooky stuff with both eyes, or his brain won't get the message that it's not so spooky after all.

■ Human hair and fingernails and horse hoofs are made from the same protein (which explains why hoof dressing works so well as a human nail conditioner).

■ Horse hoofs grow approximately ¼ inch per month, taking almost a year to grow from coronet band to ground.

■ The height of a horse is measured at the withers because the distance from the withers to the ground remains the same (provided the horse is standing square on level ground). If horses were measured to the tops of their heads, the measurement would change every time.

■ A hand is 4″ because that was considered to be the width of an 'average' man's hand across the knuckles.

■ In ancient Egypt the basic unit of measurement was the cubit (about 20″). This was divided into "fingers" (or "digits") (about ¾″), which were grouped into 4 "palms" of about 3″ each. A "palm" plus a "digit" equaled 5 "digits" — or one "hand".

■ Adult male horses generally have 40 teeth; females, 36.

■ Alfalfa is thought to be the first cultivated forage fed to horses by humans, probably the Parthians, sometime before 100 b.c. (See military section for more about the Parthians.)

■ Barley is thought to be the first grain to be domesticated, and probably the first to be fed to horses.

■ A 1,000 pound horse produces 1,500 Btu of heat per hour (36,000 Btu/day) and exhales 2 gallons of water daily. Which is why stables need to be well ventilated, but don't need to be heated (except in "human only" areas like tack rooms, lounges, etc.).

■ The "horse box" — or horse trailer, as we know it — was invented in England in 1836 by Lord George Bentinck. Drawn by six horses, it was invented for the purpose of getting his race horses from one track to the next in a rested condition. Previously, horses had been hacked between race tracks.

■ There were no horses in Australia until 1788.

■ In 1872, Leland Stanford (1824–1893) made a bet that at one point in the gallop, all four legs of the horse are off the ground at the same time. He was proved right when Eadweard Muybridge (1830–1904), using a series of 24 cameras, photographed a racehorse called Sallie Gardner.

Muybridge Photo Sequence

■ The sequence of the horse's footfalls at the walk was correctly described by Aristotle (384–322 b.c.) in the 4th century b.c.

■ William Cavendish (1592–1676) described the trot and the amble. Claude Bourgelat (1712–1777) was the first to record the difference between the canter (3-beat) and the gallop (4-beat), but he got the sequence wrong. Etienne-Jules Marey in 1872 was the first to publish an article on the correct sequence of movements at the canter. The gallop wasn't firmly known until Eadweard Muybridge's photographs of 1872.

■ The name "Philip," and its femminine variant, "Philippa," mean "lover of horses."

■ Political humorist Will Rogers (1879–1935) had a horse named Soapsuds.

■ The state animal of New Jersey is the horse.

■ In 1917, C.G. Good of Iowa (owner of Brooklyn Supreme) paid $47,000 for a 7 year old Belgian stallion called Farceur. ($47,000 went a lot further in those days.)

■ Hippocrates (460–337 b.c.e.) is more associated with human than animal medicine, even though his name means "horse-master."

■ The state of Wyoming has used a cowboy on a bucking bronco motif on its license plates since 1936. Current Kentucky license plates show a mare with her foal and the twin towers of the Churchill Downs grandstand. As of 1992, Hawaii issued license plates to horse-drawn wagons.

■ Cars with horse names: Ford's Mustang, Pinto, Bronco; Dodge's Colt.

■ One horsepower = 746 watts; one metric horsepower = 736 watts. The horse's importance in the development of transportation and motive power is reflected in this measurement of power. The term "horsepower" was coined by James Watt, who wanted a unit of measurement for his steam engine that would be readily understood.

- Football teams with "equine" names: Indianapolis Colts; Denver Broncos.

- Horsemeat is considered a delicacy in many countries outside the U.S., especially in France. Unfortunately, much of this foreign demand is met with American supply. Some of the horses sent to slaughter are stolen; many have been discarded because they didn't win enough, or weren't fancy enough, or someone got tired of them. Efforts are underway to secure more humane transport and slaughter conditions.

- In 732, Pope Gregory III "barred horse meat from the Christian table." (Gies, p.47) While this injunction was observed in England, it was ignored in Europe, where horses no longer able to work were eaten.

- In Japan, there are restaurants specializing in horsemeat. When served raw, it is called "cherry blossom."

- Maryland has almost as many Thoroughbreds as Kentucky and twice as many as any other state.

- As of 1991, 2% of American households owned horses. This puts them (the horses, not the American households) 5th in popularity after dogs, cats, birds and fish.

- As of 1993, Moscow (Russia) is again using mounted police. The mounted police unit was first formed in 1918.

- The number of horses and mules on farms rose from 7.8 million in 1867 to 25 million in 1920, when the decline due to motor vehicles began. In 1884 there were approximately 15.4 million horses in the U.S. In 1987, there were approximately 6.6 million horses in the U.S. By 1991, that number dropped to 4.9 million.

- 27 million people ride a horse in the U.S. each year.

- Horses represent a $15.2 billion industry in the U.S. (1992 figures).

- Selective horse breeding has been practiced by the Arab tribes since at least the 7th century. Scholars believe it may have been established on the Arabian peninsula as early as 5,000 b.c.

- As a child, Caroline Kennedy (b. 1957; John F. Kennedy's [1917–1963] daughter) had a pony called Macaroni. Her brother John (b. 1960) had a pony called Leprechaun.

- Halls of Fame:
  The Horse Racing Hall of Fame, Saratoga Springs, NY.
  The National Cowgirl Hall of Fame, Hereford, TX.
  The Rodeo Hall of Fame, Oklahoma City, OK.
  The Show Jumping Hall of Fame, Tampa, FL.
  The Trotting Horse Hall of Fame, Goshen, NY.

- There is an International Horseshoeing Hall of Fame, but it is an annual awards program without a physical "hall."

- The ancient Chinese names for the wheelbarrow they invented were the "gliding horse" and the "wooden ox."

- A "furlong" — the measurement used at race tracks — is from the British "furrow-long," the standard length of a farmer's field. A furlong = 220 yards. One mile — the distance around most racetracks = 8 furlongs, as 1 furlong = 1/8 mile.

- British villages: Horsey; Donkey Town. The name of the Scottish town Horsburgh means "brook of the horses." Places named Horseford were so called because they were at fords which could only be crossed on horseback. Horsfield means "horse pasture."

- Oklahoma has an annual Festival of the Horse. Maryland has a yearly Fall Horse Festival. Virginia has a yearly Horse Festival.

- At the lateral gaits — pace and rack — the horse's back remains level, making for a more comfortable ride without the need to post. Pacers were earlier known as amblers, and are known throughout the world as early as the 4th century b.c.

- The horse industry is the largest agricultural industry in Maryland.

- Black Jack was the riderless horse at John F. Kennedy's funeral (25 Nov. 1963). The boots reversed in the stirrups indicated a fallen leader who would ride no more, a tradition tracing back to the ancient Mongols.

- Motorized vehicles are prohibited on the Greek island of Hydra. All horse-power is provided by horses and ponies.

- Horses have been depicted on the coins of many countries, particularly in the ancient world. Race horses, war horses, chariot horses have all been shown, as were mythological horses and heros, rulers, gods, and goddesses. Many of the horses shown on coins are of the type now called Arabian. Some modern (20th century) coins feature horses, primarily as the mounts of kings and generals.

- Research has shown that, when trailering horses, they are more secure and comfortable if they can ride facing the rear of the trailer.

- A bone in the human inner ear is called the stirrup.

- The forward seat, the basis of modern "English" riding, was developed by Frederico Caprilli of Italy.

- Major Harry D. Chamberlain, who helped introduce the forward seat to American riders (military and civilian), was a graduate of the U.S. Military Academy (Mounted Service School), the French Cavalry School at Saumur, and the Italian Cavalry School at Pinerolo.

- The French cavalry school at Saumur was founded in the reign of Louis XV.

- Manhole covers were originally designed with raised surfaces to keep horses from slipping.

Breed Trivia

■ Many people believe that the Arabian is the oldest pure horse breed in the world. It's probably true.

■ Most breeds of horse have 18 ribs, 6 lumbar bones, and 18 tail vertebrae. Arabians tend to have 17 ribs, 5 lumbar bones, and 16 tail vertebrae. Probably because of this, the Arabian Horse Registry of America claims that the Arabian is a distinct sub-species.

Chief Comanche, a purebred Arabian gelding, 14.2 hands, 17 years old at the time of the photo. This horse, a great-great-grandson of Skowronek, shows typical Arabian conformation. Owned and loved by the author, who also took the photo.

■ The Godolphin Arabian had a cat called Grimalkin as a constant companion. This horse was sometimes called the Godolphin Barb. He was foaled around 1725, and died in 1753.

- The Darley Arabian was bought by Thomas Darley in 1710. A 15.2 hand bay with 3 socks and a blaze, the stallion's original name was Ras-el-Fedow, "the headstrong."

- According to the Jockey Club-published American Stud Book (first 10 volumes), between 1760 and 1906, 45 Arabian stallions and 21 Arabian mares were imported to America.

- Approximately 90% of all Thoroughbreds can trace back to Eclipse, a stallion brought to England in the early 1700s. Eclipse was so named because he was foaled during a solar eclipse (1 April 1764). He died in 1789. Eclipse, a liver chestnut with a blaze and one hind stocking, was by Marske, out of Spilette by the Godolphin Arabian.

- The purebred Arabian stallion Ranger (later known as Lindsay's Arabian) was imported to Connecticut in 1765 and later purchased by George Washington to improve his horses.

- Horse breeding in Japan was influenced by the importation of Arabians in the 16th century and again in 1867, by Napoleon III in exchange for silkworm eggs. Thoroughbreds are a more recent import.

- Lord Lonsdale's Monkey, a horse of "Eastern breeding," was imported to Virginia in 1747. By the time of his death seven years later, he had sired 300 American foals.

- In 1817 the Janow Podlaski state stud (Arabian horses), Poland, was established by decree of Tsar Alexander I of Russia. In 1967, on the stud farm's 150th anniversary, Poland issued a set of eight postage stamps to commemorate the occasion. The stamps showed portraits of the stallions Ofir and Skowronek, and Arabs performing in dressage, flat racing, harness racing, polo, show jumping, and cross-country jumping.

- Skowronek (foaled 1909) was brought to England as a three-year old, to serve as a painter's model, but was bought by Lady Wentworth in 1913 and used as head stud at Crabbet for many years. Through his sons *Raseyn, *Raffles, and Naseem, Skowronek is found in the pedigree of literally thousands of champion Arabians in America. His influence has also been felt in Russia and Egypt.

Skowronek on a Polish stamp, Scott #1481. Author's collection.

■ Nedjme, one of the horses exhibited by Turkey at the 1893 Chicago World's Fair, became foundation animal No. 1 in the Arabian Stud Book. The Turkish delegation exhibited 45 Arabians at this "World's Columbian Exposition."

■ Witez II, a purebred Arabian foaled 1938 at Janow Podlaski Stud Farm in Poland, was one of the horses rescued by General George S. Patton in World War II. Beginning in 1945, Witez II stood at stud in the U.S. for many years. Witez II died in 1965, and was honored on a Polish postage stamp that year.

■ The Byerly Turk may have been an Akhal-Teke. This horse was one of the foundation sires of the Thoroughbred breed. He was obtained by Col. Robert Byerly in 1683.

■ The Arabian Horse Club was incorporated in 1908.

■ As of 1994, there were over 504,000 horses registered with the Arabian Horse Registry of America.

■ Breed standards for the Arabian call for a height of 14.1 to 15.1 hands, a weight of 800 to 1,000 pounds.

■ Registered Arabians may have no more than 17 characters, including letters, spaces and dashes, in their name.

■ Ten horses have contributed slightly more than half the genes found in the modern Thoroughbred. They are:

> Godolphin Arabian
> Darley Arabian
> Curwen Bay Barb
> Byerley Turk
> Bethell's Arabian
> White Darcy Turk
> Old Bald Peg (a mare)
> St. Victor Barb
> Lister Turk
> Leeses Arabian

The first four have contributed almost a third of the genes.

■ Recent research indicates that "native mares" had less influence on the development of the Thoroughbred than did "mares of eastern breeding."

■ Prior to 1760 no Thoroughbreds were imported to New England. The first Thoroughbred imported to the U.S. was Bulle Rock, who arrived in Virginia in 1730. Between 1730 and 1760, Thoroughbred stallions were imported to New York and Pennsylvania (one each), Maryland (3), South Carolina (4), and Virginia (14).

■ The first Thoroughbred stallion in Kentucky was Blaze. He was foaled in England, shipped to Virginia in 1793 and to Kentucky in 1797. His stud fee was $12.

- Registered Thoroughbreds may have no more than 14 letters in their name.

- The General Studbook for Thoroughbred horses was first published in 1791, in England, by James Weatherby.

- The T'ang breed of horse was developed in China during the T'ang Dynasty (618–907), by crossing many different types of horses until the type was fixed. The T'ang horse is known through many artworks.

Figurine in the T'ang Dynasty style. From the People's Republic of China. Author's collection.

- The Naragansett Pacer was the first breed developed in the United States, in the Rhode Island area. The ancestry of this breed is said to trace to either the Scottish Galloway pony or the Irish Hobby. It was in demand as a plantation horse throughout the West Indies and the American colonies.

- A stallion called Snip is considered the foundation sire of the Naragansett Pacer. Most Naragansett Pacers were about 15 hands high, of sorrel or chestnut color.

- One factor in the extinction of the Naragansett Pacer was highway improvement, and the consequent change in fashion from pacers to trotters.

■ The dams of three of Justin Morgan's foals were Narragansett Pacers, as was the dam of American Saddle Horse progenitor Gaines Denmark (1851). Narragansetts were imported to the West Indies in the 1600s to power the sugar mills. Prior to the American Revolution, New England was the major horse-breeding area of the colonies.

American Breeds stamps, Scott #2158a. Author's collection.

■ The Quarter Horse was developed in part from Irish hobbys brought to Virginia in 1666.

■ The first Quarter Horses were developed in Virginia. Due to the heavily wooded terrain, and the winding roads which followed the path of least resistance, it was difficult to find a straight road more than a quarter-mile long. Horses were raced over the quarter-mile straightaways, giving rise to the breed's name.

■ The Thoroughbred Janus is considered a foundation sire of the Quarter Horse. He was imported in 1756.

■ Printer (1795–1828), the earliest Quarter Horse to be designated a foundation sire by the American Quarter Horse Association, is considered to be the founder of the bulldog strain of Quarter Horse.

■ Steel Dust, foaled in Kentucky or Illinois in 1843, was a major Quarter Horse sire. He was taken to Texas at age three. This 15 hand, 1200 lb. bay, part Thoroughbred, was considered the fastest horse in the west in the 1850s.

■ The American Quarter Horse Association was founded in 1940.

■ In 1983, in Texas, a Quarter Horse mare who had been bred to a jack gave birth to a mule colt and a horse filly. As far as is known, this is a unique occurrence.

■ The late pro wrestler Andre Rene Roussimoff (1947–93) — better known as Andre the Giant — raised Quarter horses on his North Carolina ranch. However, at 7 ft. 4 inches, 520 pounds, it's highly unlikely he actually rode any of them...

■ Judging by the number of registrations, the Quarter Horse is the most popular breed in the world. The rarest breeds are the Caspian and the Skyros.

■ The American Quarter Horse Association spends about $5 million yearly to promote the breed.

■ The Norwegian Fjord horse is one of the national symbols of Norway. The Fjord horse has been bred in Norway for 2,000 years.

■ The birthplace of the Lipizzan breed, the Lipizzaner Stud at Lipizza (Lipica), was founded by Archduke Charles in 1580. It was destroyed, with all 90 of the resident horses, in 1992, during the war in the former Yugoslavia.

■ Lipizzans are born dark and turn white as they age. A few keep their dark coloring for life.

■ Many of the Lipizzan bloodlines were lost during World War II, and more are likely to be lost in the war in the former Yugoslavia. The six extant (as of 1993) stallion lines are Siglavy (dating back to 1765); Conversano (1767); Pluto (1772); Maestoso (1773); Favory (1779); and Neapolitano (1790).

■ A Lipizzan stallion given to the U.S. Government by Austria in 1964 was used by the Old Guard's Caisson Platoon, the "White Horse Team," based at Ft. Meyer, Virginia. They were given ten American-bred Lipizzans in 1981.

- Modern Andalusians and Fresians are similar in appearance to medieval war horses. At least, some people think so.

- The American Saddle Horse Breeders Association was formed in 1891.

- In 1908, the American Saddle Horse Breeders Association named Denmark (foaled 1839 in Kentucky) as sole foundation sire of the breed — despite the fact that the breed existed before the foundation sire did.

- The Shetland Pony, smallest pony breed, tends to be larger in the U.S. than the U.K. The harsh climate of the Shetland Isles has also produced such diminutive breeds as the Shetland Sheepdog and the Shetland Deer.

Man holding Shetland foal.

- The original Justin Morgan — the horse, not the man — was 14 hands high. (The man was probably a bit taller.) This bay horse was foaled in 1793 in Massachusetts, and lived in Vermont from age two until his death in 1821. The cause of death was neglect after being kicked.

- The dam of Justin Morgan may have been three-quarters Dutch and one-quarter Arabian. Many of the mares he was bred to were likely part Arabian.

- The Morgan Horse was named the state animal of Vermont in 1961.

- Morgans were in large part responsible for the extinction of the Naragansett Pacer, being a stronger and more versatile breed.

- Shetland ponies were first imported into the U.S. in 1885.

- The American Shetland Pony Club was founded in 1890, two years before Britain's Shetland Pony Stud Book Society.

- Buffalo Bill Cody bred Shetland ponies.

- Miniature horses have been bred for centuries as novelties for royalty. The were found in the far east as early as 3000 b.c. Today's minis can be housebroken and taught numerous tricks. They are allowed to be a maximum of 34″ tall for registration; smaller is better as long as good proportions are maintained.

- Minis were used in coal mines in England and Northern Europe as early as 1765, in much of the U.S. through the 1930s, and in West Virginia and Ohio as late as the 1950s. In the 1960s the Regina Winery in Cucamonga, California, used imported Falabellas (Argentine miniatures) to pull a specially-built stagecoach as a promotional gimmick.

- Miniatures today are bred for pets, for show, for driving — they can pull a cart with three or four adults. In trail classes they are led, and they're used in costume classes the same way. There are shows just for miniatures. They can be entered in open shows in horse classes only, not pony classes. They often win driving classes against full-size horses.

■ There are also miniature donkeys and mules.

■ Caspian ponies probably existed in Mesopotamia in 3000 b.c.

■ There are only a few hundred Caspian ponies left in the world. At one time considered a national treasure of Iran, these small horses were destoyed in large numbers when Ayatollah Khomeni came to power. Resembling Thoroughbreds, Caspians have one fewer chromosome than other horse breeds. The stallion Jehan, one of only a small number of Caspians in North America, died in December 1993 at age 31.

■ The Clydesdales became the Anheuser-Busch symbol on April 7, 1933.

■ Anheuser-Busch has three teams of Clydesdales, each based in a different part of the country.

- The Przewalski horse *(Equus przewalski)* was one of the first animals bred in captivity for the specific purpose of conservation. In the early years there was a lot of inbreeding, as well as the introduction of domestic horse genes. The most visible external sign of the latter is a chestnut coat color. Chestnut does not occur naturally in the Przewalski. An ongoing breeding effort has been working to recreate as nearly pure a strain as possible. This effort is taking place in zoos all over the world.

- The first studbook for the Przewalski horse was established in 1959 in Prague, Czechoslovakia, where it is still maintained.

- The Przewalski horse is the only true wild horse in the world today. It was named for the Polish General Przewalski (sometimes spelled Przevalski), who sent the skull and hide of the previously unknown horse to the Academy of Sciences in St. Petersburg in 1881. (Although Polish, he was serving in the Russian army at the time.) The Przewalski horse is light dun to bay with a dorsal stripe, upright mane (like a zebra) and no forelock. They stand 12.2 to 14.2 hands.

- Przewalskis have been kept and bred in captivity since 1899, and may be extinct in the wild. As of the early 1990s there were about 500 in captivity, and cooperation among the zoos owning them is helping to reduce inbreeding.

- The Przewalski horse is very similar in appearance to horses in prehistoric cave drawings. It is almost impossible to domesticate.

- John Bull, physician to Peter the Great, recorded a sighting of the Przewalski — which he called the Mongolian wild horse — in 1719.

- The Tarpan is a primitive equine which became extinct a hundred years ago. It was recreated in the 1920s by two German brothers, Heinz and Lutz Heck. The took German and Polish pony breeds and bred them back until they got the external appearance of the tarpan. X-rays confirmed the skeletal appearance was the same. The recreated tarpan breeds true.

- Tarpans stand about 13 hands high. They are dun with a dorsal stripe and a bi-color, semi-erect mane. The tail is also bi-color. Some striping is often evident on the lower legs. The tarpan is sometimes called the European Forest Horse.

- The Pennsylvania Dutch once bred a draft horse type called the Conestoga.

- Cleveland Bays were originally known as "chapman horses," because they carried the loads of chapmen (travelling salesmen).

- The Appaloosa Horse Club was founded in 1938.

- The name "appaloosa" comes from the Palouse River which flows through Oregon, Washington and Idaho. From 'a palouse horse,' to 'appalouse,' the name ended up 'appaloosa.'

- The Icelandic Pony is naturally gaited. Their unique gait is called the tølt.

- No horses or ponies have been brought into Iceland in 800 years, and any Icelandic pony who leaves is not allowed back in.

- The American Mustang Association was founded in 1962.

- The Palomino Horse Breeders Association of America was founded in 1941.

- The Pony of the Americas is a breed which looks like a pony version of the Appaloosa. The breed was established in 1956 from foundation sire Black Hand, who was by a Shetland Pony out of an Appaloosa mare.

- The American Shire Horse Breeders Association was formed in 1885.

- The Standardbred Stud Book was established in 1871.

- The Tennessee Walking Horse Breeders Association was formed in 1935.

- The foundation sire of the Tennessee Walking Horse is Black Allen (foaled 1886), by Allendorf, a trotting horse, out of Maggie Marshall, a Morgan mare.

- The Welsh Pony Society of America was founded in 1946.

- The Welsh Pony is noted for its jumping ability, many being able to jump almost their own height.

- The Akhal-Teke horse of the Central Asian desert stands about 15–16 hands, with long ears, neck and legs; it tends to be narrow through the chest. These horses are noted for the metallic sheen to their coats, particularly evident in a deep gold color said to be unique to the breed.

Akhal-Teke horse on postage stamp from Azerbaijan. Author's collection.

Tack &
Clothing Trivia

- The word "tack" is a shortened form of "tackle," meaning "equipment." The long form is still found in the phrase "fishing tackle."

- The first spurs were large thorns bound to the foot. When spurs started to be made of other materials, they included the arms through which the straps or chains are threaded to hold the spur to the foot. The Romans used a prick spur. The rowel spur appeared in the 13th century, and in some form is still used today. There is one type of spur being made today which uses adjustable tension in the metal to hold the spur on without straps or chains.

- In Paris in the 1300 there was a Guild of Spur-Makers.

- Gilded spurs were the symbol of knighthood.

- The fillis-style stirrup was named for James Fillis, a riding instructor in the Imperial Russian Army. He was active in the late 1800s–early 1900s.

- The western saddle and chaps were adapted from the Mexicans. The western or cowboy boot evolved from the high cavalry boot.

- The button-down shirt collar came from British polo players in the 1890s. They fastened down the collars to keep them from flapping up in their faces as they played. The style was adopted and popularized by Brooks Brothers Clothiers.

- The most popular "western" or "cowboy" hat was invented by a Philadelphia, Pennsylvania man, John B. Stetson, in the 1860s.

■ By 1860 the side-saddle was basically the same as the ones used today. The side-saddle is said to have been introduced to England in the 14th century by Anne of Bohemia.

■ The western sidesaddle as it's known today was developed by Col. Charles Goodnight (who appears on a 1994 U.S. postage stamp) and saddler Charles Gallop in the 1890s.

■ The type of harness used on oxen choked horses. Horses could only pull light loads until the development of the rigid, padded horse collar. This was developed by Asian nomads during ancient Roman times, and appeared in Europe during the Middle Ages. The padded horse collar increased the pulling power of the horse to as much as five times what it had been. The nailed iron horseshoe arrived the same way at about the same time. The earliest text reference to the horse collar is in a late ninth century Norwegian work, while the first picture of it in Europe is an illumination in the Trier Apocalypse from about 800. The Bayeux Tapestry (circa 1080) shows horses pulling a harrow, the first time they're shown with an agricultural tool.

■ The U.S. Army adopted the McClellan saddle, designed by George B. McClellan, in 1858.

■ The saddle was developed around 700 b.c. by the Scythians. It had no stirrups. Stirrups which held the big toe only were developed in India around the 2nd century b.c. A full-foot stirrup is found on Chinese saddles of the 4th century c.e. Turkish soldiers brought the stirrup to Hungary, and it spread from there to the rest of Europe. (It's quite possible that 'Turkish' is a misinterpretation, and that it was the Turkmenes of what is now Turkmenistan who made the introduction.) At first the stirrup was valued more for its help in mounting than its aid to rider stability: "The words for stirrup in Old High German, Old

Saxon, and Old English all derived from words for climbing."
(Gies, p.55) (I wasn't much more than 3' tall when I started
riding, and never rode anything smaller than a medium pony till
I was full grown. I climbed a lot of stirrup leathers in my time!)

■ The first (human) shoes to routinely have heels were riding
boots, because heels helped secure the foot in the stirrup.

■ Bits — the first being a kind of snaffle — were made of hide,
bone or wood before being made of metal. By 450 b.c., a single-
jointed snaffle was being used which was almost identical to the
single-jointed snaffle of today. Early bits were developed in Asia
and the East.

■ The curb bit was developed in Europe in the Middle Ages, as
was the rowled spur.

Myth, Legend Superstition & Folklore

- In Scottish rivers and lakes there lives the kelpie or water horse — *each usige* in Gaelic — a malignant water spirit who generally takes the shape of a horse. It convinces humans to get on its back, then plunges into deep water where it devours them at its leisure. It is very fond of children. Kelpies live in lochs and rivers. Loch na Dubhrachen, on Skye, is the traditional gathering place of kelpies. Possession of a kelpie's bridle grants the power of second sight. One line of thought holds that Nessie, the Loch Ness Monster, is really a kelpie with ideas above her station.

- Another water spirit — this one restricted to salt water — is the nuckelavee. It is described as half man and half horse, with a breath like pestilence and no skin on its body. It cannot cross fresh running water.

- 'Off the Isle of Man lives the shoopiltee. Its habits are like that of the kelpie, except it appears as a pony rather than a horse, and goes into the sea, rather than fresh water.

- A coltpixie is a spirit horse which lures mortal horses into bogs.

- In Japanese myth, the horse was the spirit inhabiting bodies of water, and horses were sacrificed to the water god.

- A Japanese water spirit called a kappa dragged humans and horses to a watery death. If it merely stole and rode a horse, the horse would never again be of any use. Monkeys were thought to be friends of horses and enemies of the kappa.

- The hippocampus is a hybrid creature, having the front half of a horse and the back half of a fish or dolphin. Poseidon used hippocampi to pull his chariot across the ocean.

■ In Jewish symbolism, the ass has a number of meanings, some of them contradictory. These include foolishness, humility, industriousness, labor, peace, miraculousness, patience, redemption, stubbornness and royalty. Asses were ridden by Saul, David and Solomon. Also, "the messiah [it] is said will ride into Jerusalem on an ass." (Frost, p.31)

■ Ancient Jewish theology described a large number of minor devils who appeared as "horses with men's faces, lion's teeth and women's hair, with crowns of gold and breastplates of iron, barbed and pointed tails." (Parker, p.36)

■ A number of horses are mentioned and/or described in the Bible, often associated with angels.

■ The horse Al Borak (The Lightning), who carried Mohammed to heaven, was one of the animals admitted to Paradise. Al Borak was milk white, with the wings of an eagle. Balaam's Ass and Mohammed's donkey, Yofur, were also admitted to Paradise.

■ Balaam's Ass — who, by the way, was female — and the serpent in the Garden of Eden are the only 2 talking animals in the Old Testament. She appears in Numbers 22:21-35.

■ There is a Roman Catholic organization called The Equestrian Order of the Holy Sepulchre.

■ Horses have several patron saints, including St. George, St. Stephen, and St. Anthony.

■ St. Eloy of Noyan (599–659) was patron saint of metal workers, goldsmiths, farriers and horses. Once, when brought a horse possessed by the devil, Eloy cut off the horse's leg, put a new shoe on the hoof, and reattached the leg. This apparently got rid of the devil.

■ St. Hippolytus ("horse destruction") lived circa the 3rd century 60 c.e. He was another patron saint of horses. His name reflects the manner of his death, tied by the feet to two horses and dragged to death.

■ Many religions depict their gods and heros riding white horses. St. George (of England) and St. Demetrius (of Greece) rode white horses.

■ St. Martin of Tours (4th century) was a patron saint of armorers, beggars, cavalry, coopers, domestic animals, girdlers, glovers, horses and horsemen, millers, innkeepers, tailors, wine merchants, and woolweavers. (My, he must have been busy!) He's usually pictured on horseback, dividing his cloak with a beggar. St. Martin is shown on a number of postage stamps from many countries.

■ Estonia's Santa Claus figure, Jouluvana, travels by horse and sleigh.

■ St. Eligius of France is patron of blacksmiths, horses, and all draft animals.

■ The dorsal stripe on a donkey's back is often crossed by another stripe at the withers, forming a cross. This cross has had superstitious meanings to Christians since the time of Jesus — some legends going so far as to say that the cross appeared on all donkeys after one carried Mary to Bethlehem. In some areas, hair from the donkey's cross is said to cure whooping cough. The method of effecting the cure is not specified.

■ Poseidon (Neptune) was the Greco-Roman god of horses as well as of the ocean, having created the horse in a contest with Athena. Her creation was the olive tree, and she was declared the winner by the citizens of the city that became known as Athens.

■ Horses were often sacrificed to Poseidon — which seems a strange way to honor someone!

■ Poseidon, whose name means "he who gives drink from wooded mountains," was also the patron of horse races and the god of earthquakes.

■ Poseidon's own horses had bronze hoofs and golden manes, and the sea became smooth before them as they drew the god's chariot.

■ ". . . Poseidon and Demeter were worshipped in horse-headed form in Arcadia." (Kirk, p. 51) They were referred to there as Hippios and Hippia, both names meaning "horsey."

■ Poseidon, in the form of a stallion, mated with Persephone, in the form of a mare, to produce Arion, a winged, speaking horse. Some stories say that Arion was not winged, merely very swift; that his dam was Demeter, Persephone's mother, not Persephone; and that he was the first horse given to man, being owned first by Hercules, then given by him to King Adrastus. Adrastus used Arion to escape the war at Thebes.

■ Poseidon is also said to be the sire of Pegasus, whose dam was the gorgon Medusa. Among Poseidon's titles were Hippius and Hippodromas (Greek hippos = horse).

■ Pegasus, the winged horse, was one of two offspring which the gorgon Medusa bore to the sea god Poseidon. The other was a human warrior. The name Pegasus derives from a Greek word for strong. He first appeared as a white stallion with gold wings. (Although there is one school of thought which says he was red because he was born of the blood flowing from the decapitated head of Medusa.)

Pegasus on an air mail stamp from Uruguay, Scott #CC30. Author's collection.

■ Where Pegasus struck the ground with his hoof, a spring appeared, which was called the Hippocrene. The water of this spring, when drunk, was the source of poetic inspiration, which has come to be symbolized by Pegasus himself.

■ Although all winged horses are sometimes called Pegasus, this is incorrect.

■ The human Bellerophon prayed to Athena (Minerva) for aid in a task. She gave him a golden bridle and told him where to find Pegasus, who came willingly to the bridle. Pegasus assisted Bellerophon in a number of tasks, until Bellerophon became arrogant, and tried to ride Pegasus to the top of Mount Olympus, home of the gods. The gods were offended; they sent a gadfly to sting Pegasus, who bucked Bellerophon off. The horse lived forever after with the gods; the man wandered, blind and crippled, until his death.

■ Pegasus carries the thunderbolts Zeus throws.

■ Neptune's (Poseidon) children Pelias and Neleus became horsekeepers. Pelias received from Poseidon skill in driving and training horses. This, combined with winged horses provided by the god, enabled him to win a race and, with it, the hand of the princess Hippodamia.

■ Achilles' horses Xanthos and Balios were born of the harpy Podarge (Swift-footed) to Aquile (Zephyrus), the west wind. Boreas, the north wind, was in the habit of taking the shape of a horse and siring fillies.

■ Hippona was a minor Greek horse goddess.

■ Some Greek gods and goddesses with a connection to horses and the ancient Olympic games:

> Hippodamia, a deified princess
> Demeter, in her guise of the mare-headed goddess
> Artemis, virgin goddess of hunting
> Poseidon, creator and patron of horses
> Ares, patron of horses, especially those used in war
> Hera, patroness of horses
> Athena, patroness of horses
> Castor and Pollux, divine charioteers
> Apollo, charioteer

■ Pluto (also known as Hades), god of the underworld, had four coal-black horses to draw his chariot.

■ A hippogriff is a hybrid creature, a cross between a horse and a griffin. The griffin itself is a hybrid, a cross between a lion and an eagle. The name hippogriff is sometimes applied to the winged horses. The hippogriff is sometimes used as a symbol of love.

■ The hippopod was another hybrid, having the body of a man and the legs and feet of a horse.

■ The centaur is a hybrid, human from the waist up, equine from the withers down and back. Their founding father was Ixion. It is said that centaurs originated in Thessaly. Most were crude and savage. Centaurs, according to some stories, had to eat two meals at each sitting — one of human food, one of horse food.

■ Chiron was a Titan, a son of Cronus. Some accounts say Chiron was turned into a centaur by Zeus; some stories say Apollo. He was quite civilized. He was noted for his wisdom and kindness, and taught archery, music and medicine. He was also known as a prophet. Chiron was the teacher of Achilles, Aesclepius, Hercules and Jason, among others. Chiron decided to die after being wounded accidentally by Hercules, and was placed by Zeus into the sky as the constellation Sagittarius. That is why this zodiac sign, called The Archer, is generally depicted as a centaur. There is also a southern constellation called The Centaur.

Medieval Sagittarius.

■ The cornflower plant, *Centurea cyanus,* is said to have received both its first name and its healing properties when it was used by the centaur Chiron to cure a wound caused by a poisoned arrow.

■ Aesculapius, a mortal who became the god of medicine and healing, was raised from infancy by the centaur Chiron.

■ One of the stories showing the savage side of the centaurs concerns the wedding of the Lapith princess Hippodameia, at which the centaurs got drunk and tried to rape all the females there. They were driven away by King Peirithous and pursued by Hercules. Chiron was not involved in this mess.

■ Hercules was killed by the poisoned blood of the centaur Nessus, incorporated into a robe given to him by his wife. Nessus had offered to carry Hercules' wife across a stream, but halfway across he tried to rape her. Hercules shot him. The centaur told the wife that his blood would act as a love-potion. She smeared it on a robe she gave to Hercules, thus unwittingly causing his death. He was burnt on a pyre — and some say taken to heaven from there — to avoid the prolonged death that the centaur's blood was causing.

■ The first U.S. rocket to use liquid oxygen and liquid hydrogen as propellants was called the Centaur. It became operational in 1966.

■ Mars (Ares) had four horses for his chariot, offspring of the North Wind and a Fury.

■ Consus, a Roman earth deity, was worshipped at harvest festivals. Horse races were a feature of these festivals, as they later became a feature of the Circus Maximus.

■ Phaëton, son of Apollo and the nymph Clymene, once tricked his father (the sun god) into letting him drive the chariot of the sun. He was unable to control the horses — a feat which Apollo himself sometimes found hard, and caused great destruction to the earth. To save the world, Zeus (Jupiter) had to destroy Phaëton.

■ The horses of Thracian King Diomedes lived on flesh. One of Hercules' labors was to take these horses to Mycenae. He calmed them enough to do this by killing the king and feeding him to the horses. They later escaped and were killed by wild beasts.

■ King Midas was given his ass's ears by Apollo because the king chose Pan as the victor in a musical contest. Midas hid the ears under a turban, and "only his hair-dresser knew for sure."

■ King Glaucus of Corinth fed his mares on human flesh. They later tore their master apart. See how important a proper diet is?

■ The Trojan Horse was built on the advice of Ulysses, to allow the Greeks to enter the city of Troy. It was huge and hollow, filled with armed men; the Greeks let on it was an offering to Minerva, and sailed just out of sight. The Trojans wanted to bring it into the city despite the warnings of the priest Laocoön: "for my part, I fear the Greeks even when they offer gifts." A Greek, Sinon, who let himself be captured, insisted that the horse was an offering, built large to prevent the Trojans taking it into the city. Which of course they did, and, after dark, Sinon released the men it hid. And the rest, as they say, is history.

■ Boreas (one of the 4 winds), in the shape of a stallion, mated with the mare Dardanus to sire 12 horses who could not be overtaken.

■ Apollo drew the sun across the sky in a chariot drawn by fiery horses. The horses who drew Apollo's chariot were Bronté (Thunder), Eos (Daybreak), Ethiops (Flashing), Ethon (Fiery), Erythreios (Red-producer), Philogeia (Earth-loving), and Pyrois (Fiery). Seven is an odd number for driving. Perhaps Apollo rotated the horses, driving a different set each day.

■ The ancient sun-god Helios had Aithon (Dawn), Erythraios (Sunrise), Lanpos (Mid-day), and Philogais (Sunset).

■ The image of the sun being drawn across the sky by firey horses occurs in a number of cultures.

■ In Greco-Roman myth, donkeys are a symbol of lust.

■ Many aristocratic families in ancient Greece claimed descent from horses, and included some form of the word hippeia in their names to indicate this.

- The honesty plant, *Lunaria annua,* was also known as the moonwort. In the Middle Ages it was believed to remove the shoes of horses who trod on it.

- Fairies not only had fairy horses, but were fond of taking mortal horses.

- Europeans of the middle ages believed that turquoise would protect horse and rider from all ills.

- To find the place where a vampire lies, a virgin boy, riding bareback on a virgin stallion, is led over the suspected burying ground. Where the horse stops and refuses to move, there the vampire lies. Traditions vary as to whether the stallion must be pure white or pure black. (This tradition was portrayed in the 1979 movie version of "Dracula.")

- Horses are considered prophetic in many cultures throughout the world, although the actual methods of revealing the prophecies vary.

- The symbolic meaning of the horse varies by culture and tradition. In Christian art, it represents courage and generosity. The swiftness of the horse is often used as metaphor for the swiftness of time, or of speed. Pride is another symbolic meaning. The "pale horse" is Death. Ninki-gal, ancient Queen of Hell, is represented as kneeling on a horse. The "red horse" is War. Mars (Ares), god of war, had horses called Fear and Terror. The "black horse" is famine. The "white horse" had many meanings — conquest, anarchy, innocence.

■ Witches sometimes transformed themselves into horses. More often they turned a victim into a horse — usually temporarily — so they'd have something to ride. This was generally done by means of a magic bridle. They also "borrowed" normal horses, leaving them with tangled manes.

■ Tangled manes are also a sign that brownies or pixies have been using a horse. These tiny creatures ride in the manes, and make knots for handholds.

■ Sometimes the Devil — or various demons — rides on or takes the form of horses.

■ Horse brasses, now strictly decorations on a horse's harness (or a human's wall), originated about 2,000 years ago as charms, against evil and for protection. The various designs of these horse charms have — or at one time had — meaning for various groups. Plastic horse brasses are merely an abomination.

■ Several belief systems sacrificed horses during various rituals, usually to ensure fertility.

■ On the island of Thera, near Crete, it is believed that the donkeys are inhabited by the souls of people in purgatory. Their penance is to toil up and down the steep, winding, thousand foot road, 20 or more times a day, carrying people and cargo. Throughout Greece, the Cyclades, Egypt and Syria, misbehaving donkeys are threatened with being sent to Thera. (Some people believe that Thera — also known as Santorini — is the site of Plato's Atlantis.)

■ It was — and still may be — a tradition among race-horse trainers to carry a frog's bone in their pocket. This derived from an ancient belief that powdered frog's bones were a powerful agent for subduing horses. No mention is made of how it was administered.

■ Goblins can communicate with insects, and love to direct them toward warm-blooded animals like horses. They also love to pester horses in person. Maybe we don't need insect spray, but goblin spray!

- The root of the Carlina thistle *(Carlina vulgaris)* was believed to give a man the strength and potency of a stallion. To get a properly effective plant, sperm from a black stallion had to be mixed with the planting soil and it had to be watered with the urine of a white mare.

- In some areas, the horse-goddess developed into a manifestation of the mother-goddess, protector of the dead as well as the living.

- In Portugal and other areas, there is a legend that says that the wind can impregnate a mare. The resulting foal is very swift, but short-lived.

- Piebalds are sometimes said to be unlucky. Various other colors and markings were also considered lucky or unlucky by various peoples. Black horses with no white on them were lucky in Spain, unlucky in France.

- Lady Godiva rode naked through the streets of Coventry to help persuade her husband to repeal his unjust taxes. Although based on a real person, she and her ride are basically a myth.

- Among the many constellations with horse-related names are:
     Auriga the charioteer
     Centaurus the centaur
     Equueleus the little horse or foal
     Pegasus the winged horse
     Sagittarius the archer (who is a centaur)
     The Unicorn
     The Horse and Rider (2 stars in the handle of the Big
          Dipper)

- In the 15th century, Abra-Melin the Mage conjured 2,000 horsemen — and, presumably, their horses — out of thin air for his patron, Frederick, Elector of Saxony.

- According to Albertus Magnus, writing in the 13th century, any stone hung from an ass's tail will stop him from braying.

- Ancient aphrodisiac: a man must take a horse's tooth, grind it to dust, and sprinkle the dust on his penis.

- Omen of a lucky (or unlucky) day: note whether your horse steps first with the right or left foot over the doorway of his stall. Right foot is lucky.

- The Moorish hero Alfatini is to return one day to save his people, riding on a green horse.

- The Earl of Mullaghmast sleeps with his men in a cave under his castle. Once every 7 years they wake and ride round the castle. They will continue to do so until the Earl's horse's silver shoes wear away.

- The Serbian King Marko slumbers with his horse Sharatz in a cavern under Mount Urvina They sometimes ride forth to help their country. "Sharatz" means "piebald." He breathed blue flames, and sparks were struck from his hooves.

- In Carolingian legend (those legends which have grown up around Charlemagne and his times), the black Arabian stallion Beiffror (also called Broiefort) was won in battle by the 7-foot tall Ogier the Dane. It was the only horse which could carry his weight. Beiffror died in single combat.

- Ogier the Dane, after being shipwrecked, found a magic castle on the isle of Avalon. His host was the fairy horse Papillon. Ogier lived there for 200 years, then went to France to help Paris against the Norman invaders before Morgan La Fay returned him and Papillon to Avalon, where they remain to this day.

- In Carolingian legend, Rabican was a horse who fed on air and was swifter than all others. His sire was the wind, and fire was his dam.

■ Bayard, from the Carolingian cycle, was strong enough to carry four grown men, swift enough to beat all other horses, and so devoted to his master that he died rather than let anyone else have use of him. His master, Aymon, had four sons. If just one mounted Bayard, the horse was of normal size. But if all four mounted, he stretched to accommodate them.

Belgian stamp showing Bayard carrying the four sons of Aymon, Scott #B385. Author's collection.

■ "Bayard" means ruddy or red-haired.

■ One story says that Bayard at one time belonged to Rinaldo, but was stolen and sold to Charlemagne.

■ A medieval French belief was that when the mistress of a high priest died, she was reincarnated as a black mare.

■ The Valkyries who took slain heroes to Valhalla rode white horses.

■ Dag, Norse god of day, was drawn in his chariot by a white horse called Skin-faxi (Shining Mane). The chariot of the moon goddess Mani was drawn by Alsvidur (The All-Swift). Greco-Roman moon goddess Diana also had a chariot and horses. Some hold that she had two white horses; others say that she had a black and a white.

■ The Norse sun-chariot was pulled by Arvak or Arra'Kur (Early-Waker) and Alsvid (All-Swift).

- The Persian goddess Ardvi Sura Anahita, source of the cosmic ocean and guardian of all the waters upon the earth, drove a chariot drawn by four horses. They were identified only as wind, rain, cloud and sleet.

- Hofvarpnir (Hoof Thrower; Hoof Flourisher) was the mount of Gna, messenger of Frigga (wife of Odin). Gna was the personification of the breeze. Hofvarpnir was described in the *Prose Edda* as "Hoof-Flourisher/whom Skinny-Sides/got by Breaker-of-Fences." He couldn't fly, but he could glide through the air.

- The Norse goddess Nott (Night) is drawn in her dark chariot by a black horse called Hrimfaxi (Frost or Frosty Mane). The morning dew was said to be the froth from his bit.

- Many European countries have a tradition or legend of the Wild Hunt, led by the Huntsman and his hounds. They cause thunderstorms, in some tales, and in others were said to foretell disaster. In some traditions, it is Woden who leads the hunt, with spirits of the dead riding behind him.

- Odin's horse Sleipnir had eight legs. (Think of the shoeing bills!) It was the offspring of a giant's stallion, Svafilfari (slippery, ice), and the trickster god Loki in the form of a mare. The giant was working on a task the Norse gods did not wish him to complete, so Loki stopped the work by taking the form of a mare and distracting the stallion.

- In German mythology the hero Siegfried rode a horse called Grane.

- The Norse god Heimdall rode his horse Gulltopp to the funeral of Balder, where Balder's horse, fully caparisoned, was burned with the body of his master. One hopes the horse was given a painless death before being burned.

- The hero Sigurd had a horse called Greyfell.

- The Norse god Frey had a horse called Blodighofi (bloody-hoof).

- In Norse myth Grani was the horse given by Odin to Sigurd the Volsung (known as Siegfried in the German Nibelungen). Sigurd rode Grani through a wall of fire to rescue Brynhild. In Richard Wagner's opera *Gotterdammerung* (1876), Grane is the horse that Brunhilde gives to Siegfried and, after his death, rides into his funeral pyre.

- There are many stories of ghostly carriages — and even hearses — drawn by spectral horses. Horses alone are sometimes seen in ghostly form, as are individual horsemen. Many ghost horses are headless, and/or are ridden by headless horsemen, such as in Washington Irving's "Legend of Sleepy Hollow."

American "Legend of Sleepy Hollow" stamp, Scott #1548. Author's collection.

- Of the 50 or so hillside figures cut into the turf of England, horses comprise the largest group.

- All the horses derive from the Uffington horse; most date from the 17th century or later.

- In England, on Uffington Hill where the soil is chalk, a great horse has been cut out of the turf — The White Horse of Uffington. It is 374 feet long and 120 feet high. It is as deep as 130 feet at one point. One theory is that King Alfred cut it to celebrate his victory over the Danes in 871, but it is likely that it is much older. It is mentioned in the records of Abingdon Abbey in 1571. The valley below the horse is — or was — called The White Horse Vale.

- The White Horse of Uffington is the best known of a number of "white horses" or hill figures in various parts of England. The features of this horse are similar to those seen on the coins of Boadicea (d. 61 c.e.), and match the description of the ancient goddess Ceridwen, who was sometimes depicted as a white mare. The Uffington Horse is simpler in design than other hillside horses, and, unlike most of them, it faces right.

- Bronze age engravings and Celtic coins of the last centuries b.c. portray horses that face right and resemble the Uffington Horse.

- Some hold that the Uffington horse is a depiction of Epona, an ancient Celtic goddess. She was the special protector of horses, especially mares and foals, and often appeared in the form of a white mare. The word "pony" comes from her name.

- An old superstition connected with the Uffington horse says that to stand in the figure's eye and revolve three times will ensure the success of a wish. Except that there's now a fence around the figure to protect it, so it's no longer possible to do this.

- The purpose of the Uffington Horse is not known.

- Many British hill figures — horses and others — are next to Iron Age hillforts.

- The Westbury White Horse is 176 feet long, 113 feet high. It is located south of Devizes, England.

- There is (or was; it may have been removed by now) a replica of the White Horse of Uffington at Flat Creek Stables and Campground in Hogansville, GA. It was created by Evan Molyneaux in the 1970s, made of concrete.

- On the Bratton Downs, five miles from Westbury in Wiltshire, is a horse more realistic than the Uffington. It's 166 ft long.

- There used to be a horse cut into the hillside at Tysoe, but it is no longer visible.

■ Quote to note: "...The word 'hobgoblin' really signifies a demon horse, though not now used in this sense. Its derivation is 'hob' from Middle English hoby, 'a small horse,' whilst goblin means 'demon' or 'malicious fairy.' " (Howey, p.36-37)

■ A hobby is a medium-sized ambling (pacing) horse. Hobby horses, the toy, are known as far back as the reign of Edward III (1312–1377) as part of May Day celebrations. They weren't really toys, nor just fake heads on a stick, but elaborate costumes. Some were just horses, some looked like a man mounted on a horse. Many of the costumes had moveable mouths, operated by a stick or string. Eventually, as with many of today's Halloween customs, what started out as innocent fun turned to nastiness, and hobbys ended up being banned from most May Day celebrations.

■ The horse has had religious significance as far back as Neolithic times. It has primarily been associated with the sun and sun gods, and with fertility — which is strange, because the horse isn't all that fertile an animal.

■ In many cultures, a king's or nobleman's horses were killed and buried with him, either as a sacrifice to the gods or for his use in the afterlife.

■ In Thrace — now Bulgaria — in the Balkans, the representation of a horseman has been found on numerous monuments — but no tombstones. Called the Thracian Rider God, he probably had a solar association, but very little is known about him. The monuments date mostly from the 2nd and 3rd centuries. They have been found as far away as Anatolia and Western Europe.

■ The Thracian Rider God was generally shown on horseback, holding a spear, in much the same position as the Christian St. George. When Christianity reached that area of Thrace, the people switched allegiance from one to the other.

■ Many books of dream symbols and interpretations claim that to dream of a stallion means sex (of the human variety). Some claim that any horse is a sexual symbol, especially if it's being ridden. A horse in general can mean violent emotion but also intellect or intelligence, as well as energy and strength. Runaway horses signify something out of control. Black horses symbolize death. Horseshoes seem to mean good luck whether you're awake or asleep.

■ A Japanese folk belief says that to dream of a red horse is to be warned of a fire.

■ According to the Talmud, any dream of a white horse is good, but to dream of a chestnut or dark horse is good only if they do not move. It is evil if they do.

■ Maryland folklore says that to dream of a black horse was always bad luck; to dream of a white horse was either good or bad — depending on who was interpreting the dream. To dream of horses at all could be a sign of death. To dream of fat horses meant good luck; of thin horses, poverty; of white horses, that you'd be getting a letter.

■ When shown in human form riding a horse, the Celtic goddess Epona usually carried a stable key. Her cult spread throughout Europe after she was taken over by the cavalry units of the Roman army as a protective goddess of horses. She was known from Britain to Northern Italy, from Spain to Eastern Europe.

■ Very similar to Epona are Irish goddesses Macha of Ulster and Medb of Connacht; and Welsh goddess Rhiannon.

■ The Welsh horse goddess Rhiannon evolved from the older Celtic/Gaulish Epona. When not depicted in the form of a mare, she was often shown sitting sideways on a horse. Epona was worshipped by the Celts of Gaul, and in Rome as Regina (the queen). Her Roman devotees were cavalrymen. She is always shown with or on a horse.

■ Epona was the daughter of a human man and a mare. She protected cows and oxen as well as horses.

■ Two heroes who helped found Kent (England) were Hengest (meaning "stallion") and Horsa (meaning "horse"). The symbol or emblem of Kent is a white horse.

■ The horse was one of several animals held sacred by the Celts.

■ The Celtic god Manannán Mac Ler ('mac' means 'son of' and Ler or Lir was a sea god) had a chariot drawn by horses who ran along the surface of the sea. One of them was called Shining (or Splendid) Mane.

■ The dark horse in British symbolism indicates uncertainty, the unknown.

■ King Mark of Cornwall (marc = horse; marach = rider) is said to have had horse's ears.

■ The Irish hero Cúchulainn had two horses, the Grey of Macha and the Black Sainglend. He both rode and drove them. Conall, in the story of Cúchlainn, had a horse called Dewey-Red.

■ Silbury — a 130-foot high flat-topped artificial hill in England, near Marlborough — is possibly the burial-mound of a knight in golden armor. Another theory holds that it is the hiding place of a solid gold statue of horse and rider.

■ The pagan Irish heaven promises unlimited horse racing.

■ Wayland's Smithy is a megalithic stone formation on the Ridgeway in Oxfordshire (formerly Berkshire), England. Wayland the Smith, invisible, still lives there. If you travel by the smithy, and your horse has lost a shoe, leave the horse and a coin. When you return in an hour or so, your horse will be shod and your coin will be gone.

■ The breeding of silk-worms in China is under the protection of a goddess known as Lady Horse-head. She was a young woman who was abducted by the skin of a stallion her father had slain (the horse had performed a service to the father and for reward wanted to marry the girl, whom he loved). A god changed her into a silk-worm before taking her to heaven.

■ In China, horses were used to defend tombs from demon attack. K'un, descendent of the Yellow Emperor Huang Ti, took the form of a white horse to dam the waters of chaos.

- According to the 1596 book *The Chinese Book of Medicine*, horses can travel at night because they have eyes on their knees. (An old name for the chestnuts on horses' legs is "night-eyes".)

- Before the Indian god Indra rode an elephant, he rode an Aryan horse. A white horse called Kalki was to be the final avatar (incarnation) of Vishnu, according to Hindu mythology.

- In Indian mythology, the horse represents Surya, the sun-god. He is sometimes said to be a white, winged horse; sometimes he is said to be drawn in a horse-drawn chariot. These were either seven mares known as the Harits (green), or one seven-headed horse called Etasha.

- In India, the creation of the horse is attributed to Vishnu.

- The Mongolian Everlasting Blue Sky God, Bei Ulgan, rode through the stars on his sky horse.

- A legend says that the Arabian horse was first bred at the time of King David of Israel (d. circa 961 b.c.).

- When Prince Siddhartha rode out of the city on the first step of his new life as Gautama Buddha (563–483 b.c.), he rode the stallion Kanthaka.

■ When Buddha lay dying, his disciples came to pay homage. Among them were 12 animals, for whom the 12-year cycle of the Asian zodiac are named. The horse was the seventh animal to arrive. The hour of the horse is that between 11 am and 1 pm. On the compass, the horse indicates the south. The sign of the horse (or any of the other zodiac animals) has different meaning depending on which of the elements is it combined with (wood, earth, metal, water).

■ In the 20th century, if you were born between the following dates, you were born in a year of the horse:

24 Jan 1906	—	12 Feb 1907
11 Feb 1918	—	31 Jan 1919
30 Jan 1942	—	4 Feb 1943
3 Feb 1954	—	23 Jan 1955
23 Jan 1966	—	8 Feb 1967
7 Feb 1978	—	27 Jan 1979
27 Jan 1990	—	14 Feb 1991

Chinese "Year of the Horse" stamp, Scott 2258. Author's collection.

■ In Japanese myth, the horse was produced from the crown of the head of the slain food goddess, Uke-Mochi. She had been killed by the moon god.

■ Similar to the story of the Chinese goddess Lady Horse-head (and probably derived from that one) comes this one from Japan: in Honshu, where it was customary for women to care for horses, a woman fell in love with her father's stallion and said that if it were a man she would marry it. She stroked his coat three times as he said this — three is a magic number. The stallion fell in love and pined away for her. When the reason for the stallion's failure became known, the woman's father became angry and killed and skinned the horse. The woman prayed over the skin for the horse's spirit, and the skin wrapped itself around her and carried her to the sky. From where she was last seen there fell black and white insects — the first silk worms.

■ In Vedic times, an ancient Hindu horse-sacrifice ritual was the Ashva-medha. It was performed only by kings, and a king who performed 100 of them would become ruler of the universe. The ritual in its entirety took a year or more (which probably explains why no king ever managed to perform 100 of them). Sometimes the horse was only symbolically sacrificed. After a horse was consecrated by priests, it wandered free for a year, followed by the king's army. If the horse entered a foreign country, its ruler had to submit or fight. If the king who followed the horse won, there would be a triumphant return, a festival, and a sacrifice.

■ Bato Kanzeon (horse-headed Kanzeon) was a Japanese Buddhist form of Avalokitesvara, the Bodhisattva of compassion, multiple goddess of mercy, guardian of horses, farm animals, and travellers. She was usually portrayed wearing a hat or crown with a horse-head on it, seated on the ground (sometimes on a horse). Bato has three faces and a miniature horse in her hair. One of her three faces is sometimes said to be a horse.

■ The Hindu storm-god Indra has a horse called Uccaihsravas ("neighing-loudly" or "long-eared").

■ In Tibetan Buddhism, the horse often found on flags is Lung-rta (wind-horse), a luck-commanding talisman symbolizing the wind.

■ Rustum, hero of the Persian epic poem *Shah Namah*, had a horse named Ruksh who saved his life on several occasions. Once Ruksh killed a lion who was stalking his sleeping master. Ruksh was the only horse who could bear Rustum's weight; the horse was as strong as an Indian elephant and as tall as a camel. It had black eyes, a long tail, hoofs like steel (whether in color or consistency is not specified), and a light-colored body with red spots.

■ In Siberian myth, Solbon is the god of horses, worshipped by the Buriat. He has a lasso in his hand as he rides through the sky. Solbon is associated with the planet Venus. Horses dedicated to Solbon are removed from secular service in the community.

■ Ishmael, "father of the Arab people," was one day about to shoot the mare Kuhaylah, mistaking it for a deer. The angel Jabrail stopped him, saying the horse was a gift from Allah. When the mare foaled, her foal was carried in a camel's saddle-bag as Ishmael and his tribe crossed the desert. When lifted out, the foal's spine was twisted from the camel's gait. Ishmael wanted to destroy it, but again was stopped by Jabrail. This is the legend behind the truth that many Arabian horses have fewer vertebrae than other horses. When the colt matured, it was bred back to its mother, and they became the parents of all Arabian horses.

■ The Persian war god Verethraghna had ten incarnations, the third of which was a beautiful white horse.

■ In Hindu myth, the horse is the symbol of Viradsh, the vital forces which rule the world. Each part of the horse represents parts of the known world. The head represents the morning; the eyes, the sun; the open mouth, natural warmth. The entire body stands for the whole year. The limbs are the seasons, with the joints of the limbs the months. The flesh represents the clouds; the mane indicates the trees; the back of the horse is paradise. The bones are the fixed stars; the blood vessels the oceans; the spleen and the liver represent the mountains. The horse's yawn is the lightning; his froth the thunder; his dampness the rain, and his neigh suggests speech.

■ Here are some Japanese myths and folk beliefs:

> At one time, it was the custom to hang the head of a horse at the entrance to a farmhouse, to act as a charm.

> The god of marriage and birth rides a horse with bells on its harness.

> Even horses will commit suicide.

> A horse's tooth rubbed on facial blemishes will make them vanish. (If the tooth is still in the horse's head, more than just the blemishes may vanish.)

■ The legend of Pecos Bill developed in the area around the Pecos River of eastern New Mexico and western Texas. This cowboy could do anything and ride anything, including mountain lions and snakes. Pecos Bill had a horse called Widow Maker whom only he could ride. The horse got its name because it killed so many men and made their wives, widows.

■ Some legends of the American Southwest say that burros are smarter than humans. It probably depends on which burro and which human you're talking about!

■ There is a tale, in the American Great Plains region, of a ghostly white horse. It is called variously The White Steed, The Ghost Horse of the Plains, The Prancing White Stallion. One of the stories associated with him tells how he protected a young girl who wandered away from her family's wagon train.

■ In the 1800s, there was a legend in New England of a man named Peter Rugg who, with his daughter, rode forever in his carriage, trying to reach Boston but doomed never to arrive. A thunderstorm always followed the apparition, even if the sky had been crystal clear. The legend doesn't say why he was so cursed, or why the thunderstorm follows him.

■ Another New England legend tells of a man named Sam Hart, who rode a race with the Devil. When Sam realized whom he was racing, he rode to the door of the nearest church. The Devil admitted defeat, and gave Sam not only his winnings, but his (the Devil's) big black horse. This horse was never beaten in any race in which Sam entered it.

■ Some old Maryland superstitions about horses: you need to count 50 white horses while on a journey or you'll have bad luck. Counting certain numbers of white horses is a charm for having a wish granted. Different groups of people had different ideas about how many white horses one needed to count. A horse neighing or pawing outside a door meant death; horses were said to have the ability to see death in the distance. Signs of rain included horses sweating in the stable and a horse turning his lips back and "grinning". Horseshoes placed under eggs would make them hatch; a bridegroom who carried a miniature horseshoe would always be lucky.

■ Old U.S. weather wisdom:

> If the hair of a horse grows long early, look for an early winter.
>
> Extreme friskiness is a sign of approaching cold weather
>
> The hair of a horse appears rough just before a rain.
>
> Before a rain horses become restless and uneasy, shying more than usual.

■ As the horse was incorporated into the cultures of the Native American peoples, legends about the horse also developed. Navahos and Apaches were among the first to obtain horses. In their legends, the gods of the Upper World (including the Sun) molded the horse from colored clay and released it on earth. In Shoshone and Blackfoot legends, horses came from under water. Piegan Blackfoot called the horse po-no-kah-mita, "elk-dog." They were as large as an elk, and could carry a pack like a dog.

■ The Cheyenne Indians believed that they could not be hurt while riding a medicine hat pinto. "Medicine hat" refers to dark markings that cover the top of the head and both ears.

■ Morzillo, one of the horses taken to Mexico by Hernando Cortez in 1519, was left with the Mayas of Lake Petèn Itzá (Guatemala) in 1524 due to lameness. They worshipped him as Tziunchani, god of rain, thunder and lightning, bedecked him with flowers, and fed him on meat and vegetables. After his death (probably a quick one of colic, with that diet!), the Maya erected a statue of Morzillo, sitting like a dog. A Franciscan friar destroyed the statue in 1618, but legend says Morzillo can still be seen in the waters of the lake.

■ The unicorn is a horselike being with a single horn in the middle of its forehead.

■ One of the first writers to describe the unicorn was Ctesias, a Greek physician who lived about 400 b.c.

■ The unicorn is one of the oldest mythological beasties known, appearing in a variety of forms in a number of cultures worldwide. The earliest legends speak of a beast who is wild and savage, but the legend was tamed by Christian myth makers, who associated the unicorn with Christ.

■ The famous series of tapestries known as "The Hunt of The Unicorn" is either a Christian allegory or an allegory of courtship and marriage. This series of seven tapestries was woven about 1500, probably in Brussels.

■ Unicorns are born without horns, and stay with their dams until their horns are fully grown.

■ The unicorn's horn is generally gold or silver, but may vary, and in some tales it is multicolored. Also called alicorn, a unicorn's horn was antidote to all poisons.

■ Sometimes the unicorn is shown with a goat's beard, cloven hoofs, and tufted tail.

■ Dr. Olfert Dapper saw a unicorn in the Maine woods in 1673.

■ Unicorns are almost always white, only rarely being of other colors. They sometimes have blue eyes.

■ In Chinese myth, the unicorn is the emperor of the quadrupeds. It symbolizes peace and prosperity. It is one of the four animals of good omen. (The others are the phoenix, the dragon, and the tortoise.) The horn on the Chinese unicorn faces to the rear.

■ Unicorns can only be captured by guile, involving the use of virgins.

■ A medieval Jewish folktale says the unicorn perished because it was too big for the ark (although there seems to have been room for elephants, giraffes, and other large beasties). Another tale says God would have let it swim behind the ark; yet another that it did, but became too tired to go on and drowned, despite resting its horn on the ark once in a while.

■ An Arab story says the unicorn loved to run elephants through, but couldn't get them off its horn. After piling up three or four dead elephants, the unicorn could no longer move and was killed by the roc (a huge bird).

■ Later myth identifies the unicorn with Christ, as well as with death and evil. Which just goes to show, a symbol can stand for pretty much whatever you want it to.

■ The ancient Arabs worshipped a horse idol called Ya'uk. In southern Arabia they called the idol Ya'bub, which means "a swift horse."

Oldest, Biggest Smallest

■ The largest horse on record is Brooklyn Supreme, a Belgian who was born in 1928 and died in 1948. He stood 19.2 hands and weighed 3,200 pounds. His shoes weighed 7½ pounds each, and measured 14″ across. He lived in Ogden, Iowa. Another 19.2 Belgian was General, but he weighed "only" 2,850 pounds. General died at age 24 in 1981.

■ The tallest horse on record is Mammoth (formerly known as Sampson), a Shire gelding. He was foaled in 1848, and in 1850 stood 21.2½ hands. He lived in Bedfordshire, England.

Draft horse. Antique French postcard showing a Percheron horse. Author's collection.

■ The tallest horse currently* living is Boringdon Black King, a Shire gelding foaled in 1984. He stands 19.2 hands. He was bred in Plymouth, England. (* as of 1994)

■ The smallest horse on record is Little Pumpkin, a stallion foaled in 1973. In 1975, he stood 14″ (that's *inches*, not hands) high and weighed 20 pounds. He is, according to published reports, well-proportioned with no dwarf characteristics. He is owned by the Della Terra Miniature Horse Farm of South Carolina.

- As of 1994, the oldest Shetland Pony in America is the 52-year-old Teddy Bear. He lives in Virginia.

- The oldest horse on record is Old Billy. Foaled in 1760, he died at age 62 in 1822. He was a draft cross bred in Woolston, Britain.

- A French pony stallion foaled in 1919 died in 1973 at the age of 54 years.

- The oldest Thoroughbred on record is Tango Duke, who was foaled in 1935. He died at age 42 in 1978. He lived in Victoria, Australia.

- An Icelandic horse named Tulle is reported to have lived to age 57.

- The oldest age at which a broodmare produced a healthy foal is 42. It was her thirty-fourth foal, born in 1933 in Australia.

Historical Trivia

■ Small carvings of horses have been found in various sites which date back 30,000 years. (see artistic and general trivia sections for more information on this.)

■ Horses were probably first domesticated around 6,500 years ago. They were first kept as food animals — a source of milk as well as meat. They were used as a general means of transportation as early as 1,000 b.c.

■ People began riding horses at least 6,000 years ago in what is now Ukraine and Southern Russia.

■ Riding may have begun on the Scythian steppes north of the Black Sea about 4,000 b.c. Archeologists deduced this from the wear marks on a horse's teeth, which they say can only have been caused by a bit. The earliest bits were probably rope or copper.

■ A Persian engraving dated c. 3000 b.c. shows a horse being ridden.

■ By the 2nd millennuim b.c., the horse had been domesticated in the Urals, China, and Northern Eurasia.

■ The oldest known sculpture of a domestic horse is 4,300 years old. It was found at Tell Es-Sweyhat, about 200 miles northeast of Damascus, in Syria. The figurine dates from about 2300 b.c., close to 500 years earlier than the area was believed to have domestic horses. Model chariots were also found. The figure is of a stallion, with detailed genitalia. One theory is that is was a fertility figure. It is three inches long and five inches high. This find shows "that the domesticated horse was well established in Mesopotamia in the last half of the third millennium B.C. and contributed to the rise of the world's first large empires." (Wilford)

■ The Sumerians used onagers as draft animals. A Sumerian mosaic of about 2100 b.c.e. shows a cart with solid (rather than spoked) wheels being pulled by onagers.

■ The Mycenaeans acquired the chariot in the middle of the 2nd millenium b.c.

■ The horse came to Egypt in the army of the Hyksos (Asiatic invaders) at the end of the Middle Kingdom (1963–1786 b.c.). Many horse burials have been discovered at a site believed to be the residence of Hyksos kings.

■ The Egyptians — the king and his highest dignitaries only — started their own horse-breeding efforts during the New Kingdom (1550–1069 b.c.). The horses were used to pull chariots as well as being ridden. Some pharaohs were so fond of their horses that they personally took care of them. Ramses II (19th dynasty, 1295–1186 b.c.) had, among others, two horses called "Theban Victory" and "Mut is Content". Pharaohs often hunted various types of game from their two-wheeled chariots.

■ Riding is depicted in Egyptian art as early as 1350 b.c.

■ The chariot as a hunting vehicle in shown in Egyptian and Mesopotamian sources, and mentioned in Chinese poetry of the Chou (Zhou) dynasty (1122–256 b.c.).

■ The Celts — a loose association of Iron Age tribes — were dominant from about the first millenium b.c. to the third century b.c. Their descendants live on in such places as Ireland, Scotland, Wales and Brittany; their legacy includes King Arthur, the Round Table, and the great chalk horses carved into British hillsides. They were highly proficient in the use of iron, developing iron rims for chariot wheels.

- Celtic warriors sometimes decapitated their enemies and hung the heads from their horses' necks.

- The Celts were basically an agricultural people, and devoted much effort to art. Their style was distinctive, and is preserved in manuscripts such as the Book of Kells. Horses were among the many animals depicted in drawings and carvings.

Modern interpretation of ancient Celtic art style. Embroidered by the author.

- Celtic remains have been found over most of modern Europe and the Mediterranean area. Women enjoyed near-equal status to men (this was also true of the Etruscan culture).

- The Celts' prowess as horsemen was renowned. Their horses were small; one modern writer says "just over a yard high at the withers" — which would put them in the range of small to medium ponies. A contemporary depiction shows the Celtic horsemen with their feet almost touching the ground. The Celts never ate horsemeat.

- Homer's Illiad, book XXIII, mentions chariot racing as part of the Greek's funeral games. Funeral games may have been a precursor of the Olympics.

- In ancient and medieval Britain, carriages were used by the ill and elderly. All others went on horseback or on foot. Women rode both aside and astride.

- Once the Hyksos were expelled from Egypt, the chariots they brought with them remained, being used for hunting as well as war. There were no organized chariot races, as the Egyptians —

as a people — were not as passionate about horses as many other peoples, including the Hyksos, Hittites, and Assyrians. Chariot races did become popular in Egypt later, during the Hellenistic period (fourth century–first century b.c.).

■ The Etruscan civilization flourished in the region north and west of Rome during the seventh century b.c. Chariot racing is depicted on many of their tombs, including one called The Tomb of the Two-Horse Chariots. These may represent funeral games as spectators and officials are also shown.

Figurine in the Classic Greek style. From USA. Author's collection.

■ Xenophon (c. 430–355 b.c.), in his *Art of Horsemanship,* gave instructions for bridling a horse virtually identical to those found in any current horse book.

■ The peoples of the Eurasian steppes were expert mounted archers. The Asian steppes produced many peoples who were superb horsemen. It was the home of trousers — much more suitable for riding than robes. The Chinese copied the Huns' trousers in 300 b.c. to fight cavalry with cavalry.

■ The Scythians were a nomadic horse-riding people of Indo-European origin. They lived in the area north of the Black Sea. Their primary treasure was gold, which they fashioned into decorated jewelry and other items. The highly complex and detailed figures on these pieces include a number of horses. For a few hundred years the Scythians ruled the area in which they lived. When a king (chieftan) died, his favorite concubine and closest servants were killed and buried with him, as were his horses, all decked out in their finest clothes and trappings. Over 300 horses have been found in a single grave. A year after a king's death, a large number of his bodyguards were strangled, along with their horses, then impaled and set in a circle around the grave. By 106 b.c. the Scythians had been wiped out by the Sarmatians, who were later wiped out by the Huns.

■ In Athens in ancient times there was a religious festival called the Panathenaia. One event of this festival was the *apobates* race, in which warriors lept back and forth between moving chariots. This event was staged in the *agora* (marketplace) into the second century b.c.

Figurine in the classic Greek style. From USA. Author's collection.

■ In 102 b.c. General Li Guang-li brought a few of the Great Horses of Ferghana (now Turkestan) to China.

■ In 1929, a dig at Pazyryk, north of Altai, discovered burial places containing horses dating back to 100 b.c. The horses were "masked as reindeer" (Grousset, p. 18). The masks and harness were decorated with animal figures.

■ According to the *Aeneid,* the Trojans had an equestrian exercise called "The Game of Troy," part of which involved filing around in interlacing circles. (Sounds like "Threading the Needle.") This exercise, with the same name, was still being performed in Virgil's (70–19 b.c.) time.

■ Ancient Romans referred to trotting horses as "successari" (shakers) and "cruciatores" (tormentors). Not surprising, considering the long miles they had to ride without stirrups.

■ According to the Greek orator Lysias, the Amazons (warrior-women) were the first to tame horses. Many of them had names reflecting this association, *e.g.* Hippolyte, "of the stampeding horses"; Hippodameia, "horse-tamer"; Lysippe, "she who lets loose the horses."

■ In ancient and medieval Britain, carriages were used by the ill and elderly. All others went on horseback or on foot. Women rode both aside and astride.

■ Among the Yakuts of the Siberian plateau, it was forbidden to strike or speak roughly to a horse.

■ The ancient Mongols fed plant roots to their horses, rather than the barley then commonly used. Children were taught to ride at as early as two or three years; women and girls were taught archery and riding along with the males. Women as well as men wore trousers, and were as skilled with horse and bow. Their spring festival was held on the ninth of May, when all white horses were gathered together and consecrated. When a great khan (lord) died, his best horses and mules were slain to serve him after death, as were any horses met on the road to the burial place. Huge herds of horses were raised, with men owning thousands of horses. The drover who looked after the horses was called an *alqashi.* He carried a long stick with a rope on it to catch horses. (This stick is shown on several Mongolian postage stamps.)

■ Among the Kirghiz nomads, "striking another man's horse or making insults against it were considered the same as striking or offending the man." (Maslow, p.51)

- In the nomadic horse tribes, the style of dress of men and women was more similar than it was in any other peoples.

- Mongols and Tartars drank a drink made of fermented mare's milk called *kumiss.*

- October Horse was the name given to the right-hand horse of the winning team of a chariot race held each October 15th in ancient Rome. The horse was sacrificed to Mars (Ares), god of war.

- The travois — a sort of triangular sledge — was the earliest form of animal-drawn vehicle. It was pulled by dogs or humans where horses weren't available.

- The Huns' ponies were described as ugly, but swift and with great endurance. The Huns were said to live on horseback.

- The Mongols were said to resemble their horses — small, stocky, heavy framed, but with great stamina and endurance. They, like the Huns before them, were mounted archers, with highly mobile cavalry. They hunted their human prey as they did game animals.

- The Arimaspi people of the eastern steppes are thought by one authority to derive their name from the Iranian *ariamaspa,* "friends of horses."

- In the Persian empire, a prince's skill at riding and hunting was seen as evidence of his fitness to rule.

- The first wide-spread postal system was during the time of Augustus Caesar (31 b.c. – 14). Messengers on horseback or in coaches carried mail along the network of Roman roads, with posts along the way to indicated the distance that must be traveled before the messenger could rest and get fresh horses. There were inns at these posts. Hence the term "post office."

- Persian horses, brought to China in Han times (206 b.c. – 22) were prized for polo, war, and the hunt. They were called Dragon Horses or Horses of Heaven. A Han emperor gave one of his female relatives in marriage to a "barbarian" king in exchange for 1,000 horses.

■ Roman emperor Caligula (12–41) lavished an ostentatious love on his horse, Incitatus. Not only did Caligula make him a senator (a consul by some reports), but the horse "hosted" parties (and woe to him who treated Caligula rather than Incitatus as the host at these events) and lived in an ivory stall with a marble manger and gold drinking vessels. He also had his own slaves and furniture.

■ When Poppaea, wife of Nero (37–68), died in 65, even the mules in her funeral procession were doused in perfume.

■ Korea had a "pony express" system started in 487 by King So Chi. It has been commemorated on a modern Korean postage stamp.

■ Ireland was noted for the quality of its horses as early as the seventh century.

■ An Arabian poet and warrior named Antar (flourished 600) was at one point given the name Alboufauris (father of horsemen) because of his skill with the horse Abjer.

■ In the seventh century in Japan, Imperial decrees covered almost every aspect of life, including how people sat on horseback. It was as this time (about 682) that Japanese women began riding astride.

■ Early aristocrats in Japan owed their high positions to their horses, as the fighting horseman was the leader of the clan.

■ In 797, horse-changing posts for royal messengers were established in France.

■ Norse settlers took horses to Greenland about 1,000.

■ King John (1167–1216) imported over 100 Flanders stallions into Britain to aid in the breeding of heavy war and draft horses.

■ Medieval baggage-carrying horses were called sumpter horses.

■ Medieval upper-class women often rode to the hunt (of various animals). Personal preference determined whether they rode astride or aside.

■ Genghis Khan's (1164–1227) personal guard consisted of 1,000 warriors on black horses. Genghis rode a white stallion.

■ Richard Plantagenet — a.k.a. Richard the Lion-Heart (1157–1199) — rode a horse called Fauvel during the Crusades.

■ King Alexander III of Scotland (b. 1249) died in 1286 when he rode his horse over a cliff during the night.

■ In Europe during the 1300s, an average day's journey on horseback was about 30 to 40 miles. Messengers often did 40 to 50 miles. In an emergency, with a change of horses, they could do 100 miles. Packtrains did about 15 to 20 miles a day.

■ During the Ming dynasty (1368–1644), Chinese tea was exchanged for nomad horses.

■ Women rode astride until the 15th century, then followed the period of the sidesaddle.

■ Joan of Arc (c. 1412–1431) rode a black stallion.

■ One of Richard III's war horses was named Blanc Sanglier, "White Boar," an allusion to one of his heraldic devices. Richard (1452–85) reigned from 1483–85.

■ During the 400 year Turkish occupation of Greece (1453–1821), only the Sultan's Imperial Cavalry were allowed to ride horses. The important place the horse had held in Greek culture was lost during this time.

■ Henry VII (1457–1509) passed an act prohibiting the export of horses from England.

- Hernando Cortez (1485–1547) conquered Mexico in the 1500s with 400–600 men and 16 horses. According to a foot soldier, Bernard Diaz, there were seven good stallions, five good mares, and four horses good for little or nothing. Cortez started out with a dark chestnut who soon died. He then acquired a dark horse called El Arriero. The Indians had never seen horses before, which was in Cortez's favor, and at first thought horse and rider were one creature. Before they learned the truth, the coastal Indians called horses Tequanes ("Monster"). The Aztecs called them Tenacamazatl ("Big Deer"). The Aztecs sacrificed captured horses as well as humans, mounting their heads on a racks outside their temples.

- Cortez's horse El Arriero became known as Morzillo. Cortez rode him on a 1524 expedition to Honduras. The horse became lame while being transported by canoe by a friendly tribe who lived on the shores of Lake Peten-Itza. He was left there, and worshipped as a god. (See mythology section for more on this horse.)

- Pignatelli's academy of horsemanship was founded in the 16th century.

- Hernando De Soto (c. 1500–1542) brought 300 horses to Florida in 1539.

- Francisco Vásquez de Coronado (1510–554) brought 250 horses to Arizona in the 1540s.

- Francisco de Santillanna, who held the title of "knight-farrier-veterinarian," was with Franciso Vásquez de Coronado (1510–1554) on his expedition to the New World in 1540–42. When Coronado set out to conquer the Seven Cities of Gold, he recruited 400 knights, each with several horses.

- According to legend, Ivan IV ("the Terrible," 1530–1584) held Turcoman, his Arabian, in higher regard than any other horse in his stable.

- The first carriage (as opposed to cart) to be built for the British monarch was built for Elizabeth I (1533–1603). (Carriages have four wheels, carts have two, although this isn't an iron-clad rule.)

- In 1564, the horse-drawn coach was introduced to England from Holland.

- In the mid- to late 1600s, New England products — including horses — were shipped to and sold in the West Indies. Some of these horses were bred by Puritans — who also raced them. Some of those Puritans weren't quite as "pure" as modern myth paints them.

- French horses were brought to Nova Scotia in 1604.

- English horses landed in Jamestown, Virginia in 1609.

- Dutch horses arrived in New York in 1623.

- Hackney coaches first appeared in London in 1625. In 1635, the speed limit on these coaches was three mph.

- Horses arrived in Massachusetts in 1629.

- ". . .[S]ometimes, as among the Angaus Bedde and Jukun of northern Nigeria, riders seem to have literally stuck themselves to their mounts by cutting the horse's back and sitting astride the blood." (Spring, p.34) (This was in the 17th–19th centuries.)

- Horse breeding was a leading industry in early New England. In 1668, the Massachusetts general court decreed that, to improve the breed, only stallions "of comely proportions and fourteen hands in stature" were allowed to run free on the town commons. All others were required to be stabled or gelded.

- The Plains Indians were expert horsemen by the 1800s.

- On March 26, 1865, Gen. (later President) Ulysses S. Grant (1822–1885) let President Abraham Lincoln (1809–1865) ride his horse, Cincinnatus. This was the only time the general let anyone else ride the horse. Lincoln was said to have ridden well.

- General U.S. Grant received two Arabian stallions, Leopard and Linden Tree, as a gift from the Sultan Abdul Hamid II of Turkey (1842–1918) in 1879. Grant was in Constantinople at the time.

- In 1825, horse-drawn buses were introduced in London. 1831 saw the first horse-drawn buses in New York.

- On September 18, 1830, The Tom Thumb — the first locomotive built in America — lost a nine-mile race to a horse. The course ran between Riley's Tavern and Baltimore, MD, and the locomotive didn't finish. Engines were called "iron horses" in the early days of the railroad.

- The first passengers on the Baltimore and Ohio railroad, in 1830, were in trains pulled by horses.

- Thomas James Smith, first marshal of Abilene, Texas, rode a horse called Silverheels. Smith tamed the town before Wild Bill Hickok arrived as marshal. Hickok, whose real name was James Butler Hickok (1837–1876) was a U.S. marshal, a soldier, and a scout. Hickok is shown on a US postage stamp.

- Wild Bill Hickok rode a horse called Black Nell.

■ In 1834, J.A. Hansom introduced his two-wheel, one-horse Hansom cab in London.

■ William Frederick "Buffalo Bill" Cody (1846–1917) worked when young as a horse wrangler and mounted messenger. Later he was a U.S. Army scout and showman, starting his first Wild West Show in 1883. He had a white horse named McKinley who followed the hearse at his funeral. He also rode a white Arabian stallion called Muson and a horse called Brigham. Buffalo Bill got his nickname from his expertise in killing buffalo.

■ Just before he was shot in the back by Bob and Charlie Ford, Jesse James (1847–1882) was dusting a framed picture of a race-horse named Skyrocket.

■ Outlaw Emmett Dalton had a horse called Katie who once belonged to Jesse James.

■ The Japanese emperor Meiji (1852–1912) had a horse called Kinkazan who lived 27 years.

■ The Pony Express lasted only 18 months, April 3, 1860 to October 24, 1861 and was a commercial failure. All 80 riders were young white men. It carried a total of 34,753 pieces of mail. From July 1, 1860 through October 24, 1861, the Pony Express carried mail under contract to the United States Post Office Department.

■ The Plains Indians of Texas had horses by the 1690s. By the 1730s horses had reached the Missouri River, and were well into Canada by the 1770s. They were spreading west at the same time. Indians first used the horse as food as well as transport.

■ The legendary English outlaw Dick Turpin (1706–1739) rode a horse called Black Bess.

■ George Washington (1732–1797) owned a horse called Blueskin. He purchased two Naragansett Pacers in 1796.

■ Paul Revere (1735–1818), silversmith and patriot, made his famous ride on April 18, 1775. William Dawes started out with Revere, at about ten p.m. (not midnight, as in the poem). No one knows for sure the name and breeding of the borrowed horse Revere rode; it may have been a Thoroughbred called Brown Beauty; it may have been a Naragansett Pacer.

■ Thomas Paine (1737–1809), author, rode Button.

■ George III (1738–1820) had 11 Masters of the Horse.

■ The first Thoroughbred born in America was foaled in 1740, by Bulle Rock out of Bay Bolton.

■ Thomas Jefferson (1743–1826) rode his favorite horse, Wild Air, to his inauguration (1801) because the coach horses which were being bought for him arrived too late.

■ Light Horse Harry Lee (1756–1818) gave an Arabian to George Washington.

■ By the mid- to-late 1700s, horses were among the most important possessions of the native peoples of the Americas.

■ For many Plains Indian tribes of the 18th century, a family's rank was determined by how many horses they possessed.

■ The Sioux Indians at one time called the horse the "holy dog."

■ At every English coronation until that of George IV (1762–1830) in 1821, the royal champion rode fully armed into the banquet hall and threw down a gauntlet to defy anyone who challenged the queen or king's right to rule. Queen Elizabeth I's (1533–1603) champion was Sir Edward Dymoke.

■ Ponies were first used in mining pits in 1763. The last four British pit ponies used in mines run by the state-owned British Coal Board were retired in February 1994.

■ Czar Nicolas of Russia had a race horse called Krepsh. It was executed in front of a firing squad.

■ In 1771 a coach trip from Boston to Portsmouth, New Hampshire, took two days. Private coaches were available for a longer time span than public ones, but to a far more limited number of people.

■ The funeral coach of President William Henry Harrison (1773–1841) was drawn by 12 white horses, with his favorite riding horse, Old Whitey, walking riderless behind.

■ President John Tyler (1790–1862) had a horse called The General.

■ In the the late 18th century, post (mail/messenger) boys began rising — "posting" — to the trot, using their stirrups as a base of support.

■ Those who long for the horse-and-buggy days might find this quote of interest: "excrement... pervaded the outdoors of the nineteenth-century city, making it a sort of equine latrine." (Furnas, p.457). The cobblestoned streets made sweeping up all the manure practically impossible.

- President Franklin Pierce (1804–1869), on horseback, once ran down a woman named Mrs. Nathan Lewis. He was arrested and later released.

- In the early 1800s, wild horse herds in East Texas were hunted for their hides.

Pony Express riders on American stamps, Scott #894 and #1154. Author's collection

- The first Pony Express rider was Johnny Frye. He left St. Joseph, Missouri, on April 3, 1860, at 7:15 a.m. William Hamilton was the last to carry the mail on the first westward trip. He arrived April 14, 1860.

- The maximum load for a Pony Express rider was 25 pounds. The Butterfield Line (Overland Mail) used coaches and carried up to nine passengers and 600 pounds of mail.

- Northern farm life in the U.S. between the Civil War and the coming of the automobile was a horse-based environment. Farmers generally had draft horses, a trotter, and saddle horses. This created a large market for all the supporting industries — hay, grain, blacksmith, saddlery, harness making, and vehicle construction. The local doctor often acted as the veterinarian.

- In the period from 1870 to 1900, wagoners (horse-drawn for the most part, rather than mules or oxen) transported all short-distance loads, and before the completion of the rail system, most long-distance haulage.

- During the height of the trail-drive era of the American West, one in seven cowboys was black. Mexicans and Native Americans were also much in evidence as cowboys.

- In the days of America's old west, an unmarked trail from Salt Lake city to the Mexican border was known as Horse-Thief Trail because it was used to move stolen horses.

- In 1875, London had to remove 1,000 tons of horse manure from its streets daily.

- File this under "I should have stayed in bed": in 1875, a thief named Dick Fellows ran into some *really* bad luck. He rented a horse to ride out and rob the stage, but the horse dumped him on his head. He stole a horse and robbed the stage going the other direction, but when he tried to put the cash box on the horse it bolted. Fellows tried to hide the box in a railroad tunnel, but he fell off an 18-foot drop and broke his leg — not to mention crushing his foot when the box fell on it. After dragging himself to a nearby farm, Fellows stole a horse who had been shod so that it was easily trailed, and he was caught. Sent to jail with a life sentence, he broke out and stole a horse which had been staked out nearby. Unfortunately, he didn't know it had been staked there because it had been eating loco weed. This horse ended Fellows' career — and his life.

■ Theodore Roosevelt's (1858–1919) son Archibald (1894–1979) had a pony named Algonquin.

■ In the pre-Civil War American South, there were a number of black horse trainers. They were slaves, but held a higher status than other slaves.

■ William Clark Quantrill had a horse called Charley.

■ President Harry S Truman (1884–1972) was the son of a mule trader.

■ The cattle drives of the late 1800s usually had a herd of 2500 longhorns herded by about 12 cowboys, with five to six horses each. The chuck wagon, carrying food and equipment, was often drawn by mules.

■ On December 5, 1888, H.P. Brown electrocuted a horse (and two calves) to demonstrate that AC current was an effective means of capital punishment. He later zapped several horses at Sing-Sing while perfecting the electric chair.

■ Belle Starr (d. 1889), female bandit of the old west, rode a mare called Venus whom she abused. Most of her crimes involved stealing cattle and horses.

■ Excerpt from 1890 census:

occupation	male	female
draymen, hackmen, teamsters	368,265	234
hostlers, stablemen (hired)	54,014	22
livery-stable owners	26,710	47
blacksmiths	209,521	60
harness & saddlemakers	42,647	833

■ In 1897, Sears, Robuck & Co. claimed to be selling one buggy — via mail-order! — every 10 minutes.

- Quote to note: ". . . in backwoods justice horse stealing was worse than manslaughter and a frequent occasion of lynching. To call a man a horsethief was the ultimate insult." (Furnas, p. 470).

- Before the development of electricity streetcars were drawn by horses or mules, and were sometimes called horsecars. The cars were on rails, reducing friction and making them easier to pull.

- Even after the automobile was invented, there was a long transition period when horse-drawn vehicles and cars co-existed, with horse-drawn vehicles slowly being replaced by motor transport.

- President Lyndon B. Johnson (1908–1973) owned an Arabian horse.

- Until the 1930s most funerals used a horse-drawn hearse. The funeral was the last horse-driven industry to be motorized.

- A horse called Genbaku Uma — "the atom-bombed horse" — survived the bombing of Hiroshima (August 6, 1945). He was given intensive care and lived into his 20s.

Knights in Shining Armor

■ King Henri II of France was killed in a tournament in 1557.

■ Although the stirrup was developed in the ninth or tenth century, knights didn't take advantage of them to stand and tilt at their enemies until the 12th century. At first they just threw their lances like spears.

■ The custom of mounting a horse from the left side began in the days when men wore swords slung along the left leg (so as to be easily drawn by the right hand). If a man wearing a sword on the left side attempted to mount a horse from the right side, nasty accidents were liable to result. Horses are more comfortable being mounted from the left only because of their training, and would likely be better off being trained to accept a rider from either side.

■ A full set of horse armor was known as a **bard**, or **bards**. A full bard was rarely used because of the weight and the way it restricted full movement. In the middle ages, a **trapper** or mail or quilted cloth comprised the whole bard. It covered the horse's head as well as the body, with openings in the head covering for mouth, eyes, and ears, and in the sides for the stirrups. Plate bards were introduced by the 15th century, and remained in use, in basically the same form, till the mid-16th century.

■ Each piece of horse armor, like each piece of human armor, had its own name:

> That part of the horse's armor which protected the head was called a **chanfron** or **shanfron**, and was connected

to the **crinet**, which protected the neck. Some chanfrons had a poll plate attached by a brass hinge.

The **peytral** protected the chest and forelegs, jutting out and sometimes shaped into curves at the lower edge to allow the horse more freedom of leg movement.

Flanchards covered the flanks. They were linked together by thongs and put on the horse before the saddle, so the saddle would help hold them in place. Armored reins and stirrup leathers were attached to the flanchards.

When speaking of armor, the **crupper** isn't the thin strap to help hold the saddle in place that we know today, but protection for the hind legs, including an upper plate, thigh pieces and a tail guard.

■ A simplified version of the bard, used throughout the 16th century, included an open or half chanfron, half crinet, armored breast plate, metal-reinforced war saddle, and crupper of light leather straps covered with metal scales.

Knights at a 16th century German tournament. Postcard from USA. Author's collection.

■ Horse (and human) armor was made at times of quilted fabric or leather as well as of metal.

■ There were specialized types of armor for combat, practice, and the joust. On ceremonial occasions, horses were often **caparisoned** — covered with decorative cloth coverings. Horse armor was generally made by the same craftsmen who made human armor, and it was decorated in much the same way.

- "Mimic combats" between cavalry groups were called **tournaments**; between individual riders, **jousts**. The **tilt**, a barrier between the opposing riders, was introduced in the 1420s to prevent the horses from colliding.

- The weight of a knight's armor has been greatly exaggerated by modern writers. Part of the reason for the "great horse" of the knighthood era was not just to carry weight, but to itself be part of the knight's weaponry. With a greater moving mass to provide more thrust, the knight could more easily drive his lance further into his enemy.

- When kings actively served as war leaders, they rode great horses (a.k.a. high horses) both so that they could see the whole of the battlefield, and so that all of their men could see them.

- King William I of England (a.k.a. William the Conqueror) was able to vault onto his horse while fully clad in armor. This was something all knights were expected to be able to do, and not an extraordinary feat.

- A full suit of plate armor weighed about 44–55 pounds, with the weight spread over the body. Knights were never winched into their saddle by crane except in fantasy (and the movies). All were able to mount their horses, dismount, run, etc. If they couldn't, they didn't get to be a knight in the first place.

- Medieval war-horses were called *destriers*, from the Latin *dextra*, "right hand." Once source says that this indicates that the horse may have been led with the right hand, or that it was trained to the right lead so as to move away from an opponent if it swerved.

- Knights rode in a line at the trot until they were fairly near their enemies before charging at the gallop. Knights who fell were generally trampled by other riders.

■ Quote to note: "Chivalry was both the code of courage and courtesy, which were the ideals of medieval knighthood, and the system of knighthood itself. The terms chivalry and cavalry share the same linguistic root, confirming that knighthood was the prerogative of the mounted warrior." (Friar and Ferguson, p.31)

■ In heraldry, the term for a rearing horse is *forcene*.

Parade armor by Kunz Lochner of Nuremberg, Germany, 1548. The man's armor weighed 5(pounds, the horse's 92 pounds. It was distributed evenly over the weight of the body. The Bashford Dean Memorial Collection, Metropolitan Museum of Art.

■ Horse armor was introduced to Japan in the Tokugawa (Edo) period (1603–1867). It took on the air of parade trappings, as Japan was at peace at that time. The chanfron, made of papier-mache or leather decorated with gilded lacquer, was shaped like a monster or dragon. The other pieces were made of molded leather, lacquered and gilded with heraldic devices and sewn onto cloth. These pieces included the crinet, crupper, tail guard and flanchards. No straps were used; the pieces were held in place with heavy red silk cords, ending in tassels.

■ Another source dates the introduction of knighthood — including metal armor — to Japan to the 10th century.

■ Horse armor used by the Asiatic peoples was usually of quilted leather, and covered only part of the body.

Military Trivia

■ Arab tribesmen rode mares into battle because they were less likely than stallions to vocalize.

■ The war chariot may have been perfected by the Hittites of Asia Minor about 1600 b.c.

■ From about 1700 b.c., for the next thousand years, the battle chariot and the chariot archer were the primary military force. Then came the era of the warhorse.

■ The horse was the major factor in the overthrow of the Egyptian Empire by the Hyksos ("shepherd kings") in about 1500 b.c. They introduced horses and horse-drawn chariots to Egypt.

■ Chariots were used in China as early as 1400 b.c., primarily as mobile command posts. They later became the primary military force.

■ The Mycenaens (1400–1100 b.c.) were the first people in Greece to use the horse-drawn war chariot, which had been developed by the Mitanni or Hittites.

■ Around 730 b.c., a Nubian army under King Piye conquered Egypt and he and his successors became pharoahs of the 25th Dynasty. Piye was the first of four pharoahs to have complete chariot teams — standing up — buried near him.

■ Until about 700 b.c., chariots were the elite of the ancient army, carrying nobles and royalty. Sometimes these men fought from chariots — which might have sharp blades projecting from wheel spokes — but often dismounted for hand-to-hand fighting.

- In ancient India, prior to 600 b.c., horses in the military were scarce, and reserved for drawing the chariots of kings and nobles.

- In the eighth century b.c., the chariot army of the Assyrian empire could travel as fast as 30 miles per day. Horses were transported by water where necessary.

- Philip of Macedon (382–366 b.c.) and his son Alexander the Great (356–323) integrated cavalry and infantry to make an effective fighting force. Philip is often credited with inventing the cavalry charge. Alexander is often credited with being the first to make effective use of a combination of cavalry and infantry.

- Philip and Alexander both personally led their men in battle. The cavalry carried ten-foot pikes which could be thrown or used as a lance or skewer. They also carried swords and both men and horses wore armor. Other types of cavalry used different types of weapons and armor. There were no stirrups yet; even "saddles" were only pads or blankets. Bridles were similar to modern ones.

- Alexander the Great's horse Bucephalus, given to him by his father, was killed in battle at age 30, in India. The city of Bucephalia was named for him.

- By 378 b.c., cavalry was eclipsing infantry. This had previously been the case in Asia, but took longer to occur in Europe. Rome learned from the example of the "barbarians" who were beating it and used more and more cavalry. This increasing dominance of cavalry was aided by the evolution of the saddle and development of the stirrup as well as development of new breeds of heavy horse. Both man and horse wore armor. "Shock tactics" took advantage of the weight of this moving mass to drive their lances through the enemy. Horse archers were used in conjunction with the lancers. Romans used mostly heavy horse archers, while Asian peoples also used light horse archers. By the fourth century, cavalry made up one quarter of the average Roman army.

- In addition to the elephants for which he is known, Hannibal (247–183 b.c.) was an able and experienced horseman.

- The ancient Magyars (Hungarians) used light cavalry bowmen, unarmored, as their primary military force, counting on mobility to carry the day.

- The term "parting shot" comes from Parthian shot, the technique of, while riding one direction, turning and firing an arrow in the opposite direction, backwards from the direction of travel, into the face of the enemy. It was developed by the Parthians, nomadic horsemen of the steppes of central Asia in ancient times.

- Short, re-curve bows were used by horseback archers. The length of the straighter long-bow made it almost impossible to use except on foot.

- The samurai code was "the way of the horse and the bow."

- In Niger, both Hausa warriors and their horses wore armor of quilted fabric. Pieces of mirror or polished metal were sometimes attached to the horses' headgear, to cause reflections that would distract and confuse the enemy. Quilted armor was also used by other African tribes.

- During the middle ages and later, farriers were attached to the cavalry of most countries. This was instead of, rather than in addition to, veterinarians. These farriers were expected to doctor the horses and, for the most part, did a lousy job.

- The pistol was developed to allow a soldier on horseback to fire with one hand (older types of guns required both hands to use). This allowed keeping one hand on the reins.

- The chariot disappeared from the Hindu military system about 500. They couldn't raise enough — or good enough — horses.

- The debut of feudal cavalry came in 732, when the troops of Charles Martel bested the Muslims in France. It was a system of exchange — a land grant in exchange for being prepared, with a horse, to fight when called. Warriors granted a fief were taking the first step to the status of knight.

■ In the 700s, cavalry became the mainstay of medieval warfare. Horses were highly valued; in one eighth century transaction, a man traded his farm and a slave for a horse and a sword.

■ William the Conqueror (born 1028) died at age 59 in 1087 from a riding accident. He didn't fall off his horse. On his way to a reducing spa in France, he and his army sacked and burned a garrison at a border town. Riding through the ruins, his horse stepped on something it didn't like and reared, driving the iron pommel of the saddle into William's stomach. The wound festered (peritonitis), and he never recovered.

■ During the period 1000–1200, there were three distinct types of cavalry:

> the horse archer (primarily Byzantine and Turkish)
> the heavy shock-action (primarily western Europe)
> light cavalry, with lance and sword.

Although the types blended to some extent, horse archers were never really used in western Europe.

■ Mongol military system, c. 1225: The Mongol "hordes" were never as large as generally depicted; they were so well trained, organized and disciplined as to perform amazing feats. Their force was entirely cavalry, and extremely mobile. The Mongol reflex bow was only slightly shorter than the English longbow — quite a feat to shoot from horseback. There were spare horses for all troopers and they would change mounts even during battle to keep the horses fresh.

■ A military elite of horse-owning aristocracy existed in Mamluk (also spelled Mameluke) Egypt (1250–1570).

■ Robert the Bruce (1274–1329) won the Battle of Bannockburn (1314) over a heavy English force by relying on the surefooted agility of the native Scottish ponies. The heavy English horses had a lot of trouble with the rough terrain.

- The battle of Crécy (August 26, 1346) marked the start of the infantry's re-emergence as the dominant military force, ending almost a thousand years of cavalry dominance.

- During the 1500s, light and heavy cavalry were both used, in varying proportions as various countries tried to determine the most effective way to use the horse. Lances and bows were being superseded by firearms, although swords were still carried. The distinction between heavy — shock-action — cavalry and light — harrassment and other other tactics — cavalry blurred over the years, but in the early 1800s again became pronounced. The early Napoleonic wars saw the high point of French cavalry, but by Waterloo, the English were dominant. By 1900, cavalry shock troops were almost never used.

- In 1540, Francisco Vásquez de Coronado led 250 mounted soldiers into the area near the Gulf of California.

- Oliver Cromwell (1599–1658) is credited with founding the principle of each soldier caring for his own horse. Prior to this, aristocratic cavalry men had servants to care for their horses.

- Revolutionary war cavalry General Richard Henry Lee (1756–1818) was known as "Light Horse Harry" Lee. He was father to General Robert E. Lee.

- The Duke of Wellington's (1769–1852) chestnut Arabian stallion, Copenhagen, was ridden by him at Waterloo (June 18, 1815). The horse died in 1836 at age 25.

- Napoleon Bonaparte (1769–1821) sometimes rode a white Arabian mare called Desiree. He usually liked to ride white Arabian stallions. He owned at least 60 white horses.

- Napoleon was a lousy horseman, having 19 horses shot out from under him.

- One of Napoleon's favorites was his grey Arab Marengo, who was captured at Waterloo (1815) and was kept in England until his death at age 38. Marengo was 22 years old at Waterloo. He was taken to England as a prize of war, and died there in 1829. His skeleton is in the National Army Museum, London, except for one hoof which was made into a snuff box.

■ On September 22, 1777, 23-year-old Tracy Richardson rode her horse Fearnaught from her family's farm in Montgomery County, Pennsylvania to the James Vaux mansion to warn George Washington of the approach of British troops.

■ Near Williamsburg, Virginia, there is a colonial mansion and plantation called Carter's Grove. In 1781, British cavalryman Banastre Tarleton was headquartered there. It is said that he rode his warhorse up the carved walnut staircase while hacking at the balustrade with his saber.

■ George Washington's white horse Lexington sank under him in deep sand at the Battle of Monmouth in 1778, and died of exhaustion. Washington then mounted a chestnut mare named Dolly. Washington was a big man, around 6'2" and 195 pounds. Washington also had a chestnut gelding called Nelson, whom he rode throughout the American Revolution. When Washington retired to Mount Vernon, he retired Nelson there, too.

■ Frontiersman and politician Davy Crockett (who preferred, and used, David; 1786–1836) once described himself as "half horse, half alligator." He also spoke of owning a racking horse.

■ In 1792, the U.S. government ordered the army to buy its horses only from Kentucky breeders.

■ Confederate Gen. Robert E. Lee's (1807–1870) iron gray gelding Traveller was originally named Jeff Davis. Traveller was foaled in 1857, and stood 16 hands high. He was probably descended from Diomed. Purchased by Lee in 1861, Traveller was the general's principal mount during the Civil War. Traveller was noted for his speed, endurance and fearlessness.

■ Civil War Confederate Col. John H. Mosby (1833–1916) had a horse named Coquette.

Antique American postcard, Robert E. Lee on Traveller. Author's collection.

■ Lee also had a mare called Lucy Long.

■ Confererate General Thomas Jonathan "Stonewall" Jackson (1824–1863) had a mare called Little Sorrel. He rode her at Harper's Ferry. After her death in 1886 she was stuffed. (Better than being stuffed before her death...). Her hide is on display at the Virginia Military Institute in Lexington, VA.

■ Civil War Union General Philip Sheridan (1831–1888) rode a horse called Winchester (former name Rienzi). Sheridan's famous ride was imortalized in a poem by Thomas B. Read ("Sheridan's Ride"). It is estimated that Sheridan rode Winchester 75 miles in one day, mostly at a gallop, as he rallied his troops to rout Jubal Early's Confederates. Sheridan was five foot 2 inches tall; Winchester was a black Morgan gelding. Sheridan rode Winchester through 85 Civil War battles.

■ In 1877, the US Army attempted to destroy all Appaloosa horses as a means of controlling the Nez Perce Indians. Luckily, they didn't succeed.

- One factor contributing to Napoleon's defeat at Waterloo (1815) was hemorrhoids. Because of hemorrhoidal pain, Napoleon was unable to mount his horse. Standing on the ground, he couldn't get an overview of the situation, and so was unable to give effective orders.

- Union General George C. Meade (1815–1872) had a horse called Baldy who was wounded twice at Bull Run (1861 and 1862), once at Antietam (1862), and once at Gettysburg (1863). The horse died in 1882. It's not specified whether Baldy was wounded twice in one of the Battles at Bull Run (also known as Manassas), or once in each battle there.

- During the Civil War, Confederate General J.E.B. (James Ewell Brown) Stuart (1833–1864) rode a horse called High Sky.

- George Armstrong Custer (1839–1876) had a bay gelding named Dandy as well as the chestnut Thoroughbred named Vic he rode at Little Big Horn in 1876.

- The Charge of the Light Brigade, a great cavalry disaster, occurred at Balaklava on October 25, 1854. It was ordered by James Thomas Cardigan, Seventh Earl of Cardigan (1797–1868), for whom the sweater is named. His charger was a chestnut named Ronald. Upon the horse's death, his head was stuffed and put on display in the Earl's home. This event (the charge, not the taxidermy) was immortalized in Tennyson's poem. The Earl died of injuries sustained in a riding accident.

- Teddy Roosevelt often sent overweight generals on strenuous horseback rides.

■ The horse that Theodore Roosevelt (1858–1919) brought to Cuba and rode up San Juan Hill in 1898 was named Texas.

■ In the Anglo-Persian War of 1856, Lt. A.T. Moore discovered the way to break an infantry formation known as "the square," which had been thought to be invulnerable to cavalry. He jumped his charger over the first two ranks of men (who were kneeling) and splatted on to the men behind. His horse died, but the horses of the men who followed him survived. The troopers of Lt. Moore's regiment went on to win the battle.

■ In 1865, when Lee surrendered to Grant, they agreed that all Confederate soldiers who owned a horse or mule would be allowed to keep it.

■ The 600 horses of Custer's 7th Cavalry were divided onto troops by color. "A" were coal blacks; "B" & "M" were piebald and mixed color; "H" were blood bays; "C" & "G" were sorrel (chestnut); "E" were grays. It didn't help him any at Little Big Horn (1876).

■ As a last-ditch effort at Little Big Horn, Custer ordered his men to shoot their horses and pile the bodies into a protective wall.

■ The only survivor of Custer's Last Stand at the Little Big Horn was a horse named Comanche, who belonged to Capt. Miles W. Keogh. He survived three major and four minor wounds, and by special order was never ridden again. He wandered free at each Army post where he stayed, and died of colic at age 30 (November 9, 1893). Comanche was at Ft. Riley, Kansas, when he died. His stuffed body was displayed at the 1893 Columbian Exposition in Chicago, and later was housed at the Ft. Riley museum. It is now on display at the University of Kansas.

■ The British army during the Boer War (1899–1902) lost 347,000 of its 518,000 horses to battle, malnutrition, disease and overwork.

■ The 1916 campaign into Mexico to capture Pancho Villa was the U.S. Cavalry's last mounted operation.

■ Beginning in 1942, the U.S. Coast Guard had mounted sailors patrolling the East, West, and Gulf Coasts of the U.S. They were known as "sand pounders." The unit was disbanded in 1944.

■ April 4, 1946 — the U.S. Cavalry was abolished as a separate service.

■ The caisson platoon based in Virginia is the Army's only ceremonial horse unit. They provide support for full ceremonial funerals — usually several a day — and march in parades. They were in the 1993 Inaugural Parade.

Horseshoes

■ Before nail-on horseshoes were invented — and in many places even after — horseshoes (or sandals) have been made of grass and leather. There were also early iron shoes that were tied on. The ancient Romans used bronze horseshoes tied on with leather straps. Nailing shoes on likely began around the second century b.c. but didn't become common until the end of the fifth century a.d. Horseshoes today are made from a wide variety of materials, including iron, steel, aluminum, titanium, and plastic.

■ The Celts were using nailed-on horseshoes by the sixth or fifth century b.c. The size of their bronze/iron shoes, with iron nails, indicates that their horses probably stood about 12–14 hands. They may have learned the art from the Asians with whom they had contact.

■ Persian mules were shod with fiber, according to Xenophon writing in 371 b.c. Nero's mules had gold plates as shoes, held on with rawhide.

■ The terms sandals, boots, and socks are more apt descriptions than shoes for early horse foot protectors. These "hippopodes" sometimes had metal plates placed inside the coverings of leather, paper, or cloth. These were tied to the legs, often so tightly that they caused considerable damage.

- Emperor Leo VI, ninth century, left a written record of a cavalryman's equipment which included "crescent-shaped iron horseshoes and nails."

- The Japanese didn't use nailed metal horseshoes until the turn of the 20th century. In the Tokugawa era they used horseshoes of twisted straw.

- Horseshoes were common by the 11th century, and by the 12th century were being mass produced.

- Horseshoes were introduced to Spain in the 13th century by the Arabs.

- In the 13th century, the Norman term "maréchal" designated a smith, and is still used for "farrier" in France. The words "farrier" or "ferrator" are much older.

- An ancient practice is putting a horse's shoes on backwards — toe to heels — to mislead a persuing enemy. It was used in the 11th century by King Alphonso in his escape from the Moorish king Ali Maymon of Toledo, Spain; in 1303 by Robert the Bruce in his escape from King Edward; and in 1530 by Duke Christopher of Wurtemburg in his escape from Emperor Charles V. And if you believe the movies, it was a common practice in the American West.

- The hall of Oakham Castle, in Britain, is decorated with horseshoes of all sizes from normal horse to gigantic. It has been the custom since Norman times for visiting noblemen to donate them in honor of the original builder, Henry de Ferrers ("worker in iron").

- The word "farrier," "one who shoes horses," comes from the Latin *ferrarius*, "iron worker."

- According to one tradition, a horseshoe nailed to the wall or door should have the heels pointing up, so the luck doesn't run out. According to Scottish tradition, it doesn't matter which side is up, because the purpose isn't to keep luck in, but to keep evil out. To be on the safe side, you might want to hang one each way.

■ Superstitions about horseshoes go back to the ancient Greeks. They believed in the magic powers of horseshoes for two reasons. One, the shoes were made of iron, a potent charm for warding off evil and the supernatural. Two, they were in the shape of the crescent moon, a potent fertility symbol.

■ The Christians invented the story of St. Dunstan, the blacksmith. He saw through the human shape the devil was wearing, and nailed shoes to his cloven hoofs in so painful a manner that the devil cried for mercy. St. Dunstan agreed, on the condition that the devil would never bother any building (or the people in the building) where a horseshoe was hung over the door. The first doorknockers were horseshoes which had moved from their traditional position to a slightly lower one.

■ Horseshoes have been associated with luck for as long as there have been horseshoes. In some areas, blacksmiths were regarded as lucky, too. The luckiest horseshoes are those found by chance. The belief that horseshoes are lucky is found worldwide.

■ A horseshoe was found carved into an 11th century Runic monument.

Artistic Trivia

- Paleolithic humans carved recognizable figures of horses — among other animals — from mammoth ivory. Horses were the animals most often found carved on Paleolithic spear throwers. Horses were often found painted on cave walls of this era (3 million–12,000 years ago). Some of these cave paintings indicate a belief in sympathetic magic, such as the arrow marks painted on a horse's flanks.

- Paleolithic images are the earliest man-made images of horses. There are more images of horses than any other animal. Many of these images depict the horse as a game animal.

- The famous Paleolithic cave art — both drawn and engraved — in Pech-Merle, France, includes two spotted horses. These do not represent Appaloosas, or other horses with spotted coats. Analysis has proven that the spots were created of different paint mixtures, applied at different times. The spots had a mystic or cult meaning. ("Exotic" coat colors — like the Appaloosa or Pinto — had a negative survival value in an animal hunted for food. These colors would make the horse more obvious, therefore more likely to be killed before reaching reproductive age.)

- Horses and bison are almost always shown together in Paleolithic cave art. Sometimes the horses are painted black. There are some depictions of the Przewalski horse which are remarkably realistic.

- Horses moving in a circular procession is a common theme in Bronze Age and Iron Age ritual art.

■ The "flying gallop" — the practice of painting/drawing horse with all four legs fully extended, forelegs to the front and hind legs to the rear — was adopted independently by the Europeans, the Bushmen of South Africa, and the Plains Indians of the U.S.

■ Leonardo Da Vinci (1452–1519) wrote a now-lost treatise on the anatomy of the horse.

■ In the 18th century, in good society, horse portraits were as important as human ones.

■ George Stubbs (1724–1806) often painted backgrounds to his horse paintings only if the patron required it. The locations of 450 paintings by Stubbs are known; he probably did many more. This great artist was self-taught. He painted a portrait of the first zebra brought to England.

■ Stubbs' masterwork in book form, **The Anatomy of the Horse**, was completed after 18 months of study and dissection. Stubbs did the text as well as the plates.

■ There were three major themes to which Stubbs devoted years of work: mares and foals; a lion attacking a horse; pastoral paintings of farm workers.

■ In addition to his other work, Stubbs is known for his enamels on Wedgwood ceramic plaques. Stubbs was a contemporary of

Wedgwood, and worked with him to develop the plaques he wanted.

■ Stubbs' portrait of the horse Whistlejacket was originally planned to have a landscape around it and George III on it — each painted by a different artist. Luckily, Lord Rockingham — who commissioned the three-artist painting — realized that the horse alone was a masterpiece, and left it as it was.

■ Stubbs' home in London is now the site of Selfridges Department Store.

■ Atop the Brandenburg Gate in Berlin, Germany, stands a sculpture called The Quadriga. Designed by Johann Gottfried Schadow (1764–1859), it depicts the goddess Nike ("Victory") in a carriage pulled by four horses. Napoleon took the statue to Paris in 1807; it was returned in 1814. The Quadriga was damaged in 1945 during World War II. It was repaired in 1950, and damaged again in 1989 when the Berlin Wall came down. It has since been repaired.

■ When George Catlin (1796–1872) rode across the American west in the 1830s to study and paint Native Americans, his mount was a pony called Charley.

■ The first series of Thoroughbred portraits in America was commissioned by Charles Henry Hall in 1822 from artist Alvan Fisher.

■ Rosa Bonheur (1822–1899) is best known for her painting "The Horse Fair" (in French, *Le Marche aux Chevaux a Paris*). It was done when she was only 30, and she did three versions of it. Bonheur rode and drove her own horses, and rode astride in an age when most women rode sidesaddle. She actually became rich from her animal paintings, and kept a variety of animals at her country estate. She also kept a wide variety of horses: Icelandic ponies, mustangs (named Clair de Lune, Andres, Apache), Bretons, Perche and Arabians. Her favorite riding horse was a mare called Margot. Bonheur worked primarily for the English market.

■ Famous "western" artist Frederic Remington (1861–1909) played football at Yale, spent two years in Kansas as a rancher and cowboy, and lived the rest of his life in New Rochelle, New York, creating his art.

■ In the 1960s a painting called "Sunset Over the Adriatic," by Boronali, was exhibited in Paris to favorable review. "Boronali" was a donkey who'd had a brush tied to his tail. The reaction of the critics when the deception was revealed is not noted. (It was probably unprintable.)

■ The emblem for the Ford Pinto was designed by Charles Keresztes, a former member of the Hungarian Equestrian Team. Early advertising for this car featured a pinto foal.

■ According to the National Archives, there are distinct meanings to the position of horse and rider in equestrian statues:

　　1) horse standing on all four legs, rider mounted, indicates the rider is a national hero.
　　2) horse with three legs on the ground, rider mounted, indicates the rider died as a result of battle injuries.
　　3) horse with two legs on the ground, rider mounted, indicates the rider died during battle.
　　4) horse in any position, rider standing beside the horse, indicates the horse was also killed.

■ One of the largest horse sculptures in the world is "The Mustangs of Las Colinas," a herd of nine mustangs running through a man-made stream. Created in bronze by Robert Glenn, the sculpture is located in Irving, Texas.

■ The Man O'War statue in Lexington, Kentucky, was sculpted by Herbert Hazeltine. Now at the Kentucky Horse Park, it long stood over Man O' War's grave on the farm where he was born and died.

■ Washington, D.C. has more equestrian sculptures than any other North American city. The earliest is the statue of Andrew Jackson (cast by Clark Mills) in Lafayette Park.

Circuses, Clever Horses & Carousels

■ Trained horses and fancy/stunt riding have been part of circuses, exhibitions, and other shows from the time such exhibitions were originated. Circus riding and classical dressage both originated in the religious aspects of equitation in the earliest days of human history.

■ Equestrian exhibitions were extremely popular in England in the mid 18th century. Englishman Philip Astley, "father of the modern circus," began outdoor trick-riding exhibitions after leaving the army in 1765. (He had been a sergeant-major in the 15th Light Dragoons.) He later expanded his operations, and in 1780, at age 37, built the first enclosed ampitheatre. He published six or seven books on horsemanship, all most likely ghost-written.

■ Equestrian exhibitions were popular in early America. John Sharp's show, in 1771, may have been the earliest by a professional. Sharp brought his Roman-riding stunts to shows in Boston and Salem, Massachusetts. In the *Pennsylvania Packet* (a newspaper) of August 15, 1785, Sharp advertised that a Mr. Poole "would mount three horses and while standing on the saddles would leap a hurdle at full speed." Mr. Poole was the first American to make a name for himself as a stunt rider.

■ The first full circus in America was probably the one presented in Philadelphia, Pennsylvania, in 1792, by the Englishman John Bill Ricketts. The feature act was his trick horse, Cornplanter.

■ Buffalo Bill's Wild West Show was popular through the late 1800s. It "recreated" scenes of the "Old West," with cowboys, Indians, cavalry, etc. In 1894, his show had over 450 horses and ponies.

- When Chief Sitting Bull (1831–1890) rode as a member of Buffalo Bill Cody's Wild West Show, he rode a horse called Gray Ghost.

- During the early 1900s, Ringling Brothers Circus advertised an act with "61 horses in one ring at one time." It must have been a big ring.

- In Japan, the circus was at one time known as *Kyokuba*, "trick-horse," as stunt riding was the first main attraction.

- A number of magicians and entertainers have performed their acts on horseback, while others have used horses as part of their act — for example, making one vanish before the audiences' eyes. Arabian horses were often used because of their beauty and intelligence.

- Almost all circus rings are 42 feet in diameter, a measurement established by Philip Astley. He figured out that a horse traveling in a ring of this diameter would lean in at the correct angle to assist the rider in performing stunts.

- The horses used in bareback acts are called "rosin-backs" (or "resin-backs"), for the substance rubbed into their coats to help the performers keep their footing.

- "Roman riding" is standing with one foot on each of two horses. Some roman riding acts used more than two horses, with the performer moving back and forth between them. Roman riders sometimes jumped over hurdles or through rings.

- "Baggage stock" is the circus term for the draft horses which pulled the show wagons between towns, or between the railroad yard and the show site.

- In Kissimmee, Florida, The Arabian Knights Dinner Theater provides a 20-act equestrian show for its patrons' enjoyment.

■ "Liberty horses" are those who work "at liberty" — not ridden or worked on a line, but trained to respond to voice commands and body language. Liberty horse troupes are generally matched in size and color, although larger troupes sometimes had several horses of each color, with the matched groups performing movements within the overall larger movements. Liberty acts have used as many as 60 horses.

■ A trained horse of Elizabethan times, Morocco, had a large repertoire of tricks, many of them more commonly associated with dogs. Morocco was mentioned by Shakespeare, Ben Jonson, and other notables of the day. Jonson also noted that Morocco and his owner, a Mr. Banks, were killed in Rome on order of the pope, who had them burned at the stake for practicing witchcraft.

■ In the late 19th century, Karl Kroll of Elbenfeld, Germany had a horse named Muhamed who was a mathematical genius. While blindfolded, the horse could add, subtract, multiply, divide and calculate cube roots. No trickery was ever discovered. Most of the "clever horses" — those who performed mathematical exploits — were found to be responding to clues given subconsciously by onlookers. The debunkers said that this meant that the horses weren't clever. Which is nonsense, really. Maybe they couldn't do square roots (I can't, either), or add, but they had to be extremely clever — not to mention sensitive and observant — to pick up these subtle clues not only from members of another species (humanity), but from members of this species with whom they were unfamiliar.

■ The history of the carousel dates back to a Byzantine equestrian game of circa 500. A French entertainment during the reign of Henri IV was called a carousel, and involved spearing rings suspended from ribbons. The machine developed to help noblemen train for this game evolved into the carousel as we know it today. The English developed a steam-powered carousel, but the ride achieved its greatest popularity (and artistry) in America.

Carousel, Disney World, Florida. Photograph by the author.

■ Early carousels were turned by hand or mule. When steam power came in, gears could be added to move the animals up and down. Outside horses are called standers, and have at least three feet on the ground. The outside surface of a carousel animal is called the romance side, and is carved and decorated more elaborately than the inside.

■ The Dentzel Carousel in Glen Echo Park, Glen Echo, Maryland, has been there since 1921. It is one of only a few still in their original location, and is undergoing restoration.

■ The Dentzel Company was the first carousel producer in America.

■ The King Arthur Carousel in Disneyland (California) has 72 horses.

Legal Trivia

■ A former mounted police officer of the Maryland National Capital Park and Planning Commission sued a psychologist who said that the officer was faking his horse phobia. The court threw out the case, but an appeals court overturned that decision. The final result of the case wasn't publicized.

■ In 1988, a Maryland resident was sentenced to 45 days in jail for drunk riding. He had been arrested in 1987 for galloping his horse down a crowded sidewalk in Ellicott City, Maryland, while sloshed.

■ In 1975, Charleston, South Carolina, passed an ordinance requiring that the horses who pull the sightseeing carriages wear diapers.

■ A 1985 law in Connecticut requires motorists to exercise extra caution around horses, including slowing and being prepared to slow even more or stop at a signal from the horse handler. This same law prohibits motorists from intentionally harassing a horse and rider/driver. There are similar laws in other states.

■ There are a lot of old, strange laws about horses still on the books in a lot of places. Some of these may have been repealed by now — and it's rare that any are enforced. But one has to wonder about the circumstances that caused some of these laws to be enacted in the first place.

■ In New York City, it's illegal to open or close an umbrella in the presence of a horse. This makes sense, as some horses are frightened by this.

- In Washington, D.C., all taxicabs must carry a broom and shovel — a leftover from the days of the horse-drawn cab.

- In Hawaii, horses can't be legally raced at night.

- In Kansas City, Kansas, an ordinance prohibits driving a horse without holding the reins.

- In Brooklyn, New York, donkeys are not allowed to sleep in bathtubs.

- In Leahy, Washington and Waterville, Maine, blowing your nose around horses is a no-no.

- California, Prescott, Arizona, and Ellensburg, Washington all prohibit riders from bringing horses into taverns or saloons. California law actually says you can't ride your horse into the tavern. California also bans horses from mating within 50 feet of a tavern. In Burns, Oregon, you can bring your horse into the bar if you pay an admission fee for him. Lourdsburg, New Mexico, prohibits mules from going into saloons, but doesn't say anything about horses or donkeys.

- Williamantic, Connecticut and Bera, Kentucky require red tail lights for horses ridden after dark. (This actually makes sense.)

- Colorado bans fishing from horseback, as do Washington, DC, and Utah. Knoxville, Tennessee prohibits riders from lassoing fish. Norfolk, Virginia says that horses aren't allowed in the Chesapeake Bay.

- Norfolk also says it's against the law to feed your horse on a city street. In Hostier, Mississippi, it's community parks where you're not allowed to feed or water the beast. If you water your horse in Clarendon, Arizona, be sure the bucket doesn't have a hole in it — those that do are illegal (not to mention impractical).

- Don't give chewing tobacco to a horse in Shelby Brook, North Carolina, or allow your horse to graze between the curb and building on any city street in Delaware.

- In Birmingham, Alabama, it's illegal to tie a horse to any of the shade trees along city streets, and in Helena, Montana, you can't tie them to fire hydrants. If you leave your car parked for over two hours at a time in Milwaukee, you've got to tie a horse to it. In Omaha, Nebraska, you can just tie your horse to the hitching post every house is required to have in front of it.

- In Springfield, Illinois, you can't legally hitch a horse or other animal to a lamp-post, or a mule to a tree. Richmond, Kentucky, prohibits hitching horses or mules to fences, trees or tree boxes, electric, telegraph or telephone poles within city limits. Duluth, Minnesota, is another place outlawing hitching horses to trees.

- Human females weighing over 200 pounds, when attired in shorts, may not legally ride a horse in Markanville, Illinois. In Raton, New Mexico, it's women wearing kimonos who can't ride horseback down a public street.

- Suffolk, Virginia, bans cars driven under their own power; only those pulled by one or more horses are allowed.

- In Iowa, you can't house a horse in one room of an apartment, and in California you can't keep one in a rented apartment. California also prohibits ponies, mules, a long list of other livestock, or poultry in an apartment or hotel. In Minneapolis, Minnesota, you can keep a mule in your apartment, but not a goat.

- In Emporia, Kansas, one of the people in a car must precede it through the city on foot and warn people so they can get their horses off the street. In St. Paul, Minnesota, a driver meeting a horse-drawn vehicle must get out and help the driver of the horse to pass the vehicle.

- Arizona cowboys watch out — it's illegal in that state to walk through hotel lobbies wearing spurs.

- In Ohio, it's against the law to call a doctor a horse doctor — even if he is one!

- Denver doesn't allow acrobats on the sidewalks, as they might scare the horses. In Fairbanks, Alaska, acrobats are probably safe on the sidewalks, but it's a misdemeanor to ride a horse or mule there. In Philip, South Dakota, it's illegal to have a horse or mule on the sidewalk whether they are ridden, driven, or led.

- And speaking of frightening the horses, Saco, Missouri, prohibits scarey hats (how does one know at which hat a horse might take offense?), and Steadfield, Michigan, bans riders from wearing masks or being unshaven.

- Fairbanks, Alaska, prohibits all racing of horses. Mississippi and Missouri don't allow racing on Sundays.

- You can't bathe your horse on the street in Charlotte, North Carolina, and in Lexington, Missouri, you can't bathe the horse in a watering trough.

- In Alabama and Franklin, Kentucky, it's illegal to trade horses — clean or dirty — after dark.

- Ada, Oklahoma, ordinance 235: it shall be unlawful for any person or persons to leave, keep, or permit, any horse, mule or mules, vehicles, wagons, buggy, automobile, except if same is provided with a grease pan. (Huh?)

- In Leahy, WA, it's against the law to ride an ugly horse. One person's ugly. . . The same law applies in Wilbur, Washington.

- In Fountain Inn, South Carolina, horses are required to wear pants at all times, while in Ft. Lauderdale, Florida, horses must be equipped with taillights and horns. Presumably they mean the type of horn which makes noise, not the type found on unicorns.

- If your horse neighs (or duck quacks, or dog barks) between 10 p.m. and 6 a.m., and you happen to be in Essex Falls, New Jersey, you can be arrested.

- In Illinois, it is within the law to arrest and prosecute horses or other animals.

- If you own a hotel in Boston, Massachusetts, you are required by law to "put up and bed down" a guest's horse.

- A Kentucky statute and its amendment: "No female shall appear in a bathing suit on any highway within the state unless she is escorted by at least two officers or unless she be armed with a club."

  "The provisions of this statute shall not apply to females weighing less than 90 pounds or exceeding 200 pounds, nor shall it apply to female horses."

- In Nebraska, motorists must send up warning red rockets and Roman candles at night when approaching a horse — which would probably frighten him more than the car! After the rockets, a scenic tarp must be thrown over the car to to conceal it from the horse and soothe him. If that doesn't work, the machine must be taken apart and the parts hidden in the grass. A similar "rule" was established in Pennsylvania many years ago by the Farmers Anti-Automobile Society.

■ Setting fire to a mule is prohibited in Maine, and in Ohio you can't set a fire under one. In Taylor, Arizona, you can't legally kick a mule — but the mule can still legally kick a human. Kentucky law says that walking behind a mule without first talking to it is contributory negligence.

■ In Minnesota, if a horse is frightened by the noise your car makes after cranking, you're responsible for any damage it does.

■ In Hillsboro, Oregon, it is unlawful to allow a horse to ride in the back seat of your car. I guess it's okay if the horse fits in the front seat.

■ In Tahoe City, California, it is illegal for cowbells to be worn by horses.

■ In Lang, Kansas, in August, you can not drive a mule down Main Street unless the mule is wearing a straw hat.

■ If you're riding a bicycle in Osceola, Michigan, and wish to pass a horse-drawn vehicle, you must first get the permission of the driver.

■ In Little Rock, Arkansas, it's illegal to frighten a horse with the kite you're flying.

■ Don't let your horse eat a fire hydrant in Marshalltown, Iowa — it's against the law. (I would really like to know what inspired this law!)

■ Virginia law says it's a no-no for any person to take any unhaltered horse, age one year or more, into any place of public worship, or permit it to accompany him there. Kentucky revised statutes say that you can only ride a female horse near a church when services are in progress.

■ A New Orleans, Louisiana, law of 1898 states: it shall be a misdemeanor for any person to hold, hitch, or fasten a stallion or any noisy animal within 80 feet of any place of public worship or during the time of Sunday school attendance in New Orleans.

■ The Mississippi code, chapter 28, section 1296 reads: Obscenity: stallion or jack not kept in public view. Any person shall not keep a stallion or jack nearer than 100 yards to a church, or in public view in an enclosure bordering on a public highway or nearer there to than 100 yards, nor shall any person stand such animals in open view of any public place, or negligently keep such an animal or suffer it to run at large. . . .

■ It's against Michigan law to use a horse or mule (or cattle) to take waterfowl.

■ In Baltimore, Maryland, any service performed by a jackass must be recorded.

■ In Columbia, South Carolina, "women of bad character" are forbidden to ride horseback in the streets.

■ In Rosario, Argentina, horses are required to wear hats in hot weather.

■ In Mikden, China, all horses must wear diapers, and drivers must empty them at regular intervals into special containers.

■ A British law states that an Englishman may not sell a horse to a Scotsman. Another British law says that harnessing a dog in place of your horse will subject you to a fine.

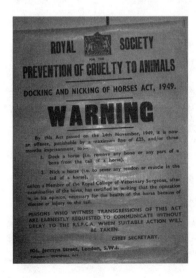

Reproduction of a notice informing the British public of a new law. From London, author's collection.

Index

All terms include their plurals (that is, to find 'mares,' look under 'mare'). Entries and page numbers in **bold type** refer to illustrations.